Middle Eastern Feasts

Michael Rantissi
& Kristy Frawley

Middle Eastern Feasts

MODERN CLASSICS FROM THE
MEDITERRANEAN TO THE ARABIAN SEA

murdoch books
Sydney | London

Contents

Introduction

Welcome to this collection of our most beloved recipes for sharing with friends and family. From the perfect hummus recipe, to abundant brunches and long lunches, along with a host of salads, condiments, cakes and more – we've brought together everything you need for a feast to remember, with recipes inspired from all across the Mediterranean, and from Türkiye to Persia and beyond.

Inside these pages are a bounty of dishes you may have tried only in a restaurant but you'll find are easily achievable at home. Along the way, this book will give you an introduction to ingredients that you may already know and love, like pomegranate, tahini, harissa, sumac and more, along with some you may not be familiar with – but once used in these recipes, you will be using them again and again in your kitchen. Try our bright chilli zhoug (page 52) as a flavour burst to your dishes, the spicy sujuk sausage in the zucchini omelette (page 14) or the tangy, fragrant chermoula with barbecued prawns (page 145).

Our signature falafel (page 35) take time to prepare but the result will be worth it and they can be scaled up according to the occasion. There are also recipes that are quick and easy to prepare with ingredients already stocked in your pantry like our Mujadarra (lentil rice) (page 137). Desserts like our Persian meringue cake (page 168) and the chocolate halva brownies (page 179) are favourites with our customers and now you can enjoy them too, and share them widely.

About Us

We're Michael Rantissi and Kristy Frawley. Together, we're the owners of Kepos Street Kitchen located in the inner Sydney suburb of Redfern. This is where we first introduced the flavours of Michael's childhood in Tel Aviv to the Sydney café scene. Since we opened KSK in 2012 it has remained a favourite for locals as well as a destination venue where people come to try our seasonal salads, dips and spice-driven dishes. Under the Kepos brand, we also owned the more refined Kepos & Co, and more recently have grown Kepos Catering to accommodate large-scale events. We have a weekly stand at the Carriageworks Farmers' Market in Eveleigh, where we stock our signature dips and salads. In 2023, we opened Salma's Canteen in Rosebery, a new-style canteen named after Michael's mother Salma, a great cook and inspiration, who loves to show her affection through food.

Brunch

We think of brunch as the most important meal of the day. In the Middle East, the classic approach is to serve a collection of dishes for people to share. You can really settle in and enjoy yourself – it's never rushed. Not only are brunch recipes usually quick and easy to make, they are also some of the most healthy and versatile dishes around. Some of these dishes are favourites from our two restaurants, Kepos Street Kitchen and Kepos & Co., and others are recipes we've been cooking for ourselves at home over the years. We hope a few of these become favourites for you, too.

SHAKSHUKA

Originating in North Africa, shakshuka has become a traditional Middle Eastern dish that every family makes – and that every family makes differently. I make my version quite spicy with more paprika and cumin coming through, but if you'd like it lighter you can reduce or omit some of the spices. You can also add greens to this dish – spinach works really well. This is a very satisfying and easy dish to make, and it can be served straight from the pan. You can make the sauce in advance, too, and reheat it when you start cooking the eggs.

4 tablespoons olive oil

1 small brown onion, diced

5 garlic cloves, diced

2 large green chillies, diced (optional)

2 large red capsicums (peppers), coarsely diced

1 tablespoon mild paprika

1 tablespoon ground coriander

1 tablespoon ground cumin

2 tablespoons tomato paste (concentrated purée)

1 kg (2 lb 4 oz) ripe tomatoes, blanched and peeled (see Note) and coarsely chopped

1 handful coriander (cilantro), leaves and stalks chopped

8 eggs

flat-leaf (Italian) parsley sprigs, to garnish

extra virgin olive oil, to drizzle

Heat the olive oil in a large ovenproof frying pan over medium heat. Add the onion and garlic and cook for 5 minutes. Add the chilli and capsicum and cook for 2 minutes. Add the paprika, ground coriander and cumin and cook for 2 minutes. Add the tomato paste and cook for 1 minute. Add the tomato and cook for 20 minutes, or until the sauce has reduced to the consistency of a tomato passata (pureéd tomatoes). Season with salt and stir through the fresh coriander.

Gently crack the eggs over the tomato sauce in the pan, spacing them out, and cover with a lid. Reduce the heat to low and cook for 3 minutes, or until the egg whites start to cook. Remove the lid, increase the heat to medium and cook for a further 3–5 minutes, until the yolks are still runny but the whites are firm. Don't worry if the eggs are not fully cooked, as the heat of the sauce will continue to cook them. Remove from the heat. Scatter over the parsley sprigs, drizzle with extra virgin olive oil, season with salt and freshly ground black pepper, and serve.

NOTE

To blanch and peel the tomatoes, score a shallow cross in the base. Put in a heatproof bowl and cover with boiling water. Leave for 30 seconds, then transfer to cold water and peel away the skin from the cross.

ZUCCHINI, SUJUK AND LABNEH OMELETTE

Excellent served for brunch or even a Sunday night dinner, this dish, which sits somewhere between an omelette and a frittata, is so easy to make. I don't think we celebrate the versatility of eggs enough – they are quick to prepare, nutritious and so much more than a breakfast food. The main ingredient in this dish is zucchini – and it may seem that there is a lot of it, but it helps to give the omelette its light, fluffy texture. The sujuk sausage adds a salty, spicy kick.

800 g (1 lb 12 oz) zucchini (courgettes), about 4 in total, coarsely grated

1 tablespoon salt

100 ml (3½ fl oz) olive oil

200 g (7 oz) sujuk sausage, diced

4 eggs

2 tablespoons labneh, plus 4 tablespoons extra to serve

3 tablespoons chopped flat-leaf (Italian) parsley

2 large handfuls mixed herbs, such as chives, flat-leaf (Italian) parsley, mint and coriander (cilantro), leaves picked

70 g (2½ oz) pine nuts, toasted

juice of ½ lemon

Put the grated zucchini in a bowl and sprinkle with the salt. Set aside until the zucchini releases its juices, about 15 minutes. Drain the zucchini, return to the bowl and set aside.

Preheat the oven to 180°C (350°F).

Heat 2 tablespoons of the olive oil in a 24 cm (9½ inch) ovenproof frying pan over medium–high heat. Fry the sujuk until crisp, then transfer to a plate and set aside. Leave the excess oil in the pan to cook the omelette.

Add the eggs, labneh, chopped parsley and half the crispy sujuk to the zucchini. Season with freshly ground black pepper and whisk to combine.

Reheat the frying pan over medium heat. Pour in the egg mixture and cook for 2–3 minutes, then transfer the pan to the oven and cook for 10 minutes, or until the omelette is done to your liking.

While the omelette is cooking, put the remaining crispy sujuk, mixed herbs, pine nuts, lemon juice and remaining olive oil in a bowl and toss to combine.

Flip the cooked omelette onto a plate and serve topped with dollops of labneh and the sujuk and herb mixture.

ASPARAGUS, PEA AND FETA TART

I think a weekend brunch is sometimes the best meal of the week because you have a little more time to prepare and a little more time to enjoy the meal. I don't get to have brunch that often at the moment because I'm usually cooking for other people at the restaurants, but it's a great way to entertain friends and family.

This tart is easy to assemble and most of the components can be made ahead of time. It looks pretty and tastes delicious and fresh. If you don't want to use peas you can use another vegetable.

350 g (12 oz/2½ cups) frozen peas, thawed overnight
grated zest and juice of 1 lemon
4 tablespoons olive oil, plus extra for drizzling
1 sheet store-bought all-butter puff pastry, about 20 x 30 cm (8 x 12 inches)
12–14 asparagus spears, peeled and trimmed
150 g (5½ oz) feta cheese
3 soft-boiled eggs
micro herbs, to garnish (optional)

NOTE
The pastry has a long cooking time. Once cut, it needs to be able to hold its shape and soak up the juices.

Preheat the oven to 190°C (375°F). Line a large baking tray with baking paper.

Put the peas in a bowl and crush them. Stir in the lemon zest, lemon juice and 3 tablespoons of the olive oil. Season with salt and freshly ground black pepper and set aside.

Put the pastry on the prepared tray and bake for about 20 minutes, or until golden brown, puffed up and very firm. Remove from the oven and set aside to cool to room temperature.

Heat a chargrill pan or a barbecue grill plate to high. Drizzle the asparagus with 1 tablespoon of the olive oil and sprinkle with salt and freshly ground black pepper. Cook for 1–2 minutes, until grill marks appear.

To assemble the tart, put the pastry on a serving board or chopping board (this will make the tart easier to cut) and top with the crushed pea mixture. Crumble the feta evenly over the tart. Tear the eggs in half and arrange them on the tart. Top with the grilled asparagus and sprinkle with sea salt and cracked black pepper. Drizzle with olive oil and scatter over micro herbs, if using.

KEPOS BENEDICT

I know this dish isn't strictly a benedict as it doesn't have the richness of the hollandaise, but you'll love the lightness of it. You can play around with the recipe as required. If you'd like to add a layer of wilted spinach or steamed leek you can. Any vegetables you add will make your day feel slightly healthier.

8 eggs
8 small slices brioche, lightly toasted
16 slices smoked salmon
mixed baby salad leaves, to serve
good-quality olive oil, for drizzling

GREEN TAHINI
2 handfuls flat-leaf (Italian) parsley,
    coarsely chopped
1 garlic clove
185 ml (6 fl oz/¾ cup) ice-cold water,
    plus more if needed
3 tablespoons lemon juice
270 g (9½ oz/1 cup) raw tahini

To make the green tahini, put the parsley, garlic and water in a blender and blitz into as smooth and fine a paste as possible. Add the lemon juice and tahini and blitz again until combined. If the mixture is too thick, add a few more tablespoons of water until it reaches the desired consistency (I like it to have the thickness of hollandaise). Season with salt, to taste.

Poach the eggs so the yolks are still runny, or to your liking.

To assemble, arrange 2 slices of toasted brioche, side by side, on each plate. Top each brioche with 2 slices of smoked salmon, a poached egg and 2–3 tablespoons of green tahini. Top with the salad leaves then sprinkle with freshly ground black pepper, drizzle with olive oil and serve immediately.

NOTE
You can serve any leftover green tahini as a dip.

BOUREKAS (MIDDLE EASTERN SAUSAGE ROLLS)

Bourekas originated in Hungary and have become a classic street food. They are traditionally served with tea-soaked eggs.

500 g (1 lb 2 oz) coarse minced (ground) beef

40 g (1½ oz) fresh or dry breadcrumbs

2 spring onions (scallions), white part and half of green part finely chopped

1 large handful flat-leaf (Italian) parsley, leaves finely chopped

100 ml (3½ fl oz) extra virgin olive oil

2 eggs, beaten, plus 1 egg, extra, beaten

2 teaspoons sea salt flakes

700 g (1 lb 9 oz) good-quality puff pastry (or 3 purchased puff pastry sheets)

2 tablespoons sesame seeds

Preheat the oven to 190°C (375°F).

Place the beef mince, breadcrumbs, spring onions, parsley, olive oil, 2 eggs and the salt in a large bowl. Season with freshly ground black pepper and mix by hand to combine.

If using a block of pastry, roll it out until 5 mm (¼ inch) thick, into sheets about 20 cm x 20 cm (8 inch by 8 inch). Cut each pastry sheet into thirds. If using purchased pastry sheets, cut them into thirds.

Brush the pastry sheets with the extra beaten egg. Put 2–3 tablespoons of the minced beef mixture along one of the long edges of the pastry. Roll into a long sausage shape, then shape like a snail shell. Repeat until you have used all of the pastry and the mince filling.

Place the bourekas onto a baking tray lined with baking paper, leaving enough room for a little spreading. Brush the tops with beaten egg and sprinkle over the sesame seeds. Bake for 35 minutes, or until golden brown. Serve with tea-soaked eggs (pictured right, see below), if desired.

TEA-SOAKED EGGS

Pour 2 litres (70 fl oz/8 cups) water into a large saucepan, add 7 English Breakfast teabags and bring to the boil. Once the water is boiling, turn off the heat and cool the water to room temperature. Carefully add 10 eggs to the water and bring back to boiling point. Boil the eggs for 5 minutes. Turn off the heat. Take out an egg and roll it on a work surface so the shell starts to crackle – this will allow the tea water to seep into the egg, giving it a lovely tan colour and a crackled appearance. Repeat with all of the eggs, return them to the hot tea (with the heat turned off) and steep for 5 minutes. Peel the eggs and put them back into the tea until ready to serve. Eat these on the day they're prepared.

HERB AND POTATO LATKES WITH POACHED EGGS AND TURKEY

Turkey meat is an underrated ingredient, and the combination of it with the crisp latkes and poached eggs works well to make a beautiful breakfast dish. Growing up in Israel, we always thought that smoked turkey was ham.

1 kg (2 lb 4 oz) desiree (all-purpose) potatoes, peeled and coarsely grated

5 egg whites

50 g (1¾ oz) potato flour

1 handful flat-leaf (Italian) parsley, leaves finely chopped

1 small handful dill, finely chopped

30 g (1 oz/¼ cup) finely chopped spring onions (scallions)

125 ml (4 fl oz/½ cup) light olive oil

8 eggs, poached

12 slices good-quality smoked turkey breast

1 handful rocket (arugula) leaves, to serve

Rinse the grated potato under cold running water to remove the excess starch and drain well. Put the potato in a tea towel (dish towel) and twist and squeeze to remove any remaining water.

Transfer the potato to a large bowl and add the egg whites, potato flour, parsley, dill and spring onion. Season with salt and freshly ground black pepper and mix well. The mixture should have a thick batter consistency.

Heat one-third of the olive oil in a non-stick frying pan over medium heat. To make each latke, drop 2–3 tablespoons of batter into the pan and gently flatten to 1 cm (½ inch) thick. Cook in batches for 2–3 minutes each side, until golden, adding more oil to the pan for each batch.

Layer 3 latkes per serve with the turkey slices, and serve with 2 eggs each and rocket leaves on the side.

MEATBALLS WITH EGGS AND LABNEH

This recipe combines two of my favourite things: meatballs and shakshuka (see page 12), and even includes some creamy labneh. This version of shakshuka is made with the more traditional tomato base. You can add crème fraîche or sour cream instead of labneh, but I find labneh a lighter option if you are serving this dish for brunch.

300 g (10½ oz) minced (ground) beef
1 egg, lightly beaten
4 tablespoons dry breadcrumbs
3 tablespoons olive oil, plus extra
    for drizzling
1 brown onion, finely diced
2 garlic cloves, crushed
400 g (14 oz) tin chopped tomatoes
200 ml (7 fl oz) chicken stock
2 tablespoons sweet paprika
1 tablespoon ground cumin
1 tablespoon ground coriander
8 eggs
4 tablespoons labneh
coriander (cilantro) sprigs, to garnish

Put the beef, egg and breadcrumbs in a large bowl. Season with some salt and freshly ground black pepper and use your hands to combine. Roll 1 tablespoon of mixture into a ball, then repeat until all of the mixture is used up. Set aside.

Heat the oil in a frying pan over medium heat and sauté the onion and garlic for 3–4 minutes. Add the tomatoes and stock, bring to the boil and cook for 5 minutes, then add the meatballs and simmer for 30–35 minutes. Add the spices, season with additional salt and black pepper and cook for a further 5 minutes.

Transfer the meatballs and sauce to a large deep frying pan. Crack the eggs into the sauce, spacing them evenly around the pan, but don't stir. Cook over medium heat for 4–5 minutes, or until the eggs are done to your liking. Remove the pan from the heat.

Dollop the labneh onto the meatballs and sauce. Garnish with the coriander, a little black pepper and a drizzle of olive oil.

NOTE
Lightly oil your hands when rolling the meatballs to give them a smooth finish.

BREAKFAST PIDE

Pide is Turkey's brilliant contribution to any menu, especially brunch. This version can be served at breakfast, lunch or dinner. The filling is up to your taste and imagination – be creative! For best results, use a pizza stone to cook the pide.

½ quantity pizza dough (page 58)
plain (all-purpose) flour, for dusting
400 g (14 oz) sujuk sausage, chopped
200 g (7 oz) grated mozzarella cheese
2 tomatoes, chopped
4 eggs

Preheat the oven to 250°C (500°F). Place a pizza stone or baking tray in the oven to heat up for at least 1 hour prior to cooking the pide.

Divide the pizza dough into quarters and roll each into a ball. Lightly flour one dough ball all over. Holding the dough with two hands, work around the dough, carefully stretching it lengthways into a long oval shape and taking care not to tear it. Shape the dough so that the centre is thinner than the crust.

Layer the pide with a quarter of the sujuk, cheese and tomato, leaving about 1 cm (½ inch) around the edge of the dough. Crack an egg onto the pide, then break the egg with your fingers and spread it over the top of the pide. Season with salt and freshly ground black pepper.

Roll in the edges of the dough to form a lip, then pinch the edges of the dough together at each pointy end to seal it, leaving some of the filling exposed.

Carefully put the pide onto the hot pizza stone or baking tray. Bake for about 3–5 minutes, until the edge of the pide is coloured and the base is cooked. Check that the bottom is cooked by lifting it up with a pair of tongs. Transfer the cooked pide to a plate and repeat with the remaining dough and toppings.

NOTE

I recommend making each pide just before you put it in the oven, rather than preparing all four at once and leaving them to sit while the others are cooking.

Clockwise from left:

*Meatballs with eggs
and labneh* (page 24),
dukkah egg salad (page 90),
Greek salad (page 113),
breakfast pide (page 25)

FISH BURGERS WITH ZUCCHINI AND DILL SALAD

A lot of home cooks are intimidated by cooking fish. This is an easy recipe to use to start practising your fish-cooking skills. The burgers make an amazing weekend treat to serve at any time of day, not just at brunch.

700 g (1 lb 9 oz) skinless, boneless snapper fillets, minced (see Note)
1 egg
3 tablespoons dry breadcrumbs
3 tablespoons chopped flat-leaf (Italian) parsley
grated zest of 1 lemon
1 teaspoon chilli flakes
3 tablespoons olive oil
4 brioche buns, cut in half
4 tablespoons good-quality whole-egg mayonnaise

ZUCCHINI AND DILL SALAD

2 small zucchini (courgettes), thinly sliced
3 teaspoons olive oil
juice of 1 lemon
1 small handful dill sprigs
2 tablespoons capers, rinsed

Put the minced fish, egg, breadcrumbs, parsley, lemon zest, chilli flakes and olive oil in a large bowl and season with salt and freshly ground black pepper. Use your hands to combine the mixture and knead it for 1–2 minutes. Divide the mixture into 4 balls and shape each into a patty. Set aside in the fridge until ready to cook.

To make the salad, combine the zucchini, oil, lemon juice, dill and capers in a bowl and season with salt and pepper.

Heat the barbecue grill plate to medium–high. Cook the fish patties for 2–3 minutes on each side, or until done to your liking.

Lightly toast the insides of the brioche buns. Spoon the mayonnaise onto the bun bases. Add some salad and a fish patty, then add more salad and finish with the bun tops.

NOTE
My preferred method of mincing the fish is using an electric mixer with a mincer attachment. Otherwise, use a sharp knife to dice the fish as finely as possible.

GREEN PEA AND RICOTTA FRITTERS

These fritters are quite versatile as they can be served for breakfast or brunch with eggs, bacon, salmon, ham or any other cold meat. At lunchtime they could be served as a side dish with a piece of steak. You can also use the mixture to make one large fritter and cut it into wedges to serve. I prefer using frozen peas in this recipe even when fresh peas are available because I find them creamier. They are also always on hand in the freezer, which makes these fritters an easy choice in the morning when I'm deciding what to cook.

500 g (1 lb 2 oz) frozen peas, thawed
100 ml (3½ fl oz) olive oil
1 small brown onion, finely diced
2 garlic cloves, crushed
4 small eggs
60 g (2¼ oz) plain (all-purpose) flour
1 large handful mint leaves,
    finely chopped
1 tablespoon dried mint
200 g (7 oz) ricotta cheese

Put the peas in a food processor and blend until lightly crushed.

Heat 3 tablespoons of the oil in a frying pan over medium heat. Sauté the onion and garlic until transparent, then set aside to cool.

Add the peas, sautéed onion and garlic, eggs, flour, fresh mint and dried mint to a large bowl and mix to combine. Season with salt and freshly ground black pepper. Fold in the ricotta in chunks, trying not to break it up too much.

Heat the remaining 2 tablespoons of oil in a non-stick frying pan over medium heat. Spoon 3 tablespoons of the mixture into the pan to make each fritter. Cook the fritters in batches for 2–3 minutes on each side, or until lightly golden.

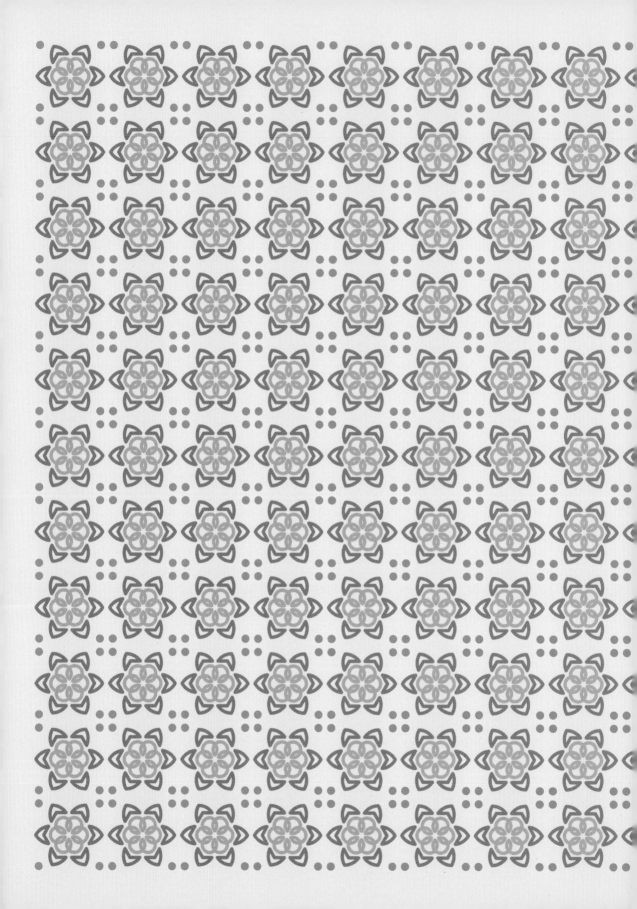

Mezze

Mezze comes from the Persian word maza, meaning 'to relish'. You'll see the word on menus all over the world, and it's eaten in homes all across the Middle East where the shared table is the way everybody gathers to eat. It stands in for a range of snacks, appetisers and small dishes designed to share. The world of mezze extends far beyond hummus, although we've included our favourite version (see page 44). We've also included a collection of light bites, skewers, hand-around food and small-but-perfectly-formed meals.

FALAFEL

It takes time to make good falafel so you'll need to start this recipe 24 hours in advance. To shape the falafel you can use a traditional falafel spoon, available at most Middle Eastern grocery stores. Alternatively, you can use two tablespoons, or do it the Egyptian way and make small patties with your hands. If you're not using a falafel spoon, you can add 2 egg whites when seasoning the mixture to make it firmer and easier to shape. However, I prefer not to add the egg whites because it's not traditional.

200 g (7 oz/1 cup) dried chickpeas

100 g (3½ oz) dried split broad beans

1 large handful coriander (cilantro), leaves picked

2 large handfuls flat-leaf (Italian) parsley, leaves picked

1 small onion, coarsely chopped

2 long red chillies, seeds removed, finely chopped

4 garlic cloves, coarsely chopped

1 teaspoon baking powder

1 teaspoon ground cumin

2 tablespoons sesame seeds

rice bran oil, for deep-frying

In a large bowl, soak the chickpeas and broad beans overnight in cold water, changing the water at least twice during this time.

Drain the chickpeas and broad beans and put them in a food processor with the coriander, parsley, onion, chilli and garlic. Whiz until grainy (not a smooth purée).

Transfer the mixture to a bowl and add the baking powder, cumin and sesame seeds. Mix together and, using a falafel spoon or two tablespoons, form the mixture into quenelles or roll it by hand into 20 patties.

Pour enough rice bran oil for deep-frying into a large deep saucepan and heat to 170°C (325°F). To test if the oil is hot enough, drop in a cube of bread and if it turns golden brown in 20 seconds you are good to start cooking. (If the oil is not hot enough, the falafel will break up.)

Working in batches, drop the falafel into the oil and deep-fry for 3 minutes, or until golden. Remove the falafel with a slotted spoon and drain on paper towel. Serve with green tahini (pictured left, see page 49) or hummus (see page 44).

ROASTED PUMPKIN WITH DUKKAH AND MINTED YOGHURT

Adding dukkah before roasting is a great way to boost the flavour of – as well as provide crunch and texture to – the humble pumpkin. It makes a great main course for vegetarians and is pretty delicious the next day if there's any left over.

1 large butternut pumpkin (squash)
100 ml (3½ fl oz) olive oil
1 teaspoon sea salt flakes
50 g (1¾ oz) hazelnut dukkah (page 46)

DRESSING
100 g (3½ oz) Greek-style yoghurt
2 tablespoons extra virgin olive oil
1 large handful mint, leaves picked
  and chopped
grated zest of 1 lemon

Preheat the oven to 190°C (375°F). Line a large baking tray with baking paper.

Cut the pumpkin into large wedges, leaving the skin on. Transfer to a large bowl with the olive oil and salt and toss to combine. Spread the pumpkin on the baking tray and sprinkle with the dukkah. Bake for 15–20 minutes, until the pumpkin is golden and tender.

Meanwhile, to make the dressing, combine the yoghurt, olive oil and mint in a small bowl and season with salt, to taste. Sprinkle the lemon zest over the top.

Arrange the pumpkin wedges on a platter and serve hot or at room temperature, with the dressing alongside.

WHITE BEAN DIP

This white bean dip is a play on a dish called musabaha, which is a chunkier hummus with a spicy, lemony flavour. The dip doesn't necessarily need the tahini, but it gives it a creamier texture and Mediterranean flavour. You can add more or less garlic and chilli for the garnish, depending on your taste.

---

300 g (10½ oz/1½ cups) dried
  white beans
1 teaspoon bicarbonate of soda
  (baking soda)
1 garlic clove, crushed
100 g (3½ oz) tahini
juice of 1 lemon
1 teaspoon salt
olive oil, for drizzling

GARNISH
1–2 garlic cloves, crushed
1–2 small fresh green chillies,
  finely chopped
juice of 1 lemon

Soak the beans in cold water for at least 8 hours, preferably overnight.

Drain and rinse the soaked beans well and put them in a large saucepan with plenty of fresh water. Cook over medium–low heat for 1½ hours, stirring occasionally and skimming from time to time. The beans will be soft but not too mushy. Add the bicarbonate of soda and cook for another 15–20 minutes, until the beans are very soft and have almost broken down. Drain the beans.

Set aside one-third of the beans. Put the remaining beans in a food processor with the garlic. Blitz to a smooth paste, then add the tahini, lemon juice and salt. Blitz again until combined.

To make the garnish, combine the garlic, chilli and lemon juice in a small bowl.

To serve, spoon the dip into a serving bowl and fold in the reserved beans. Sprinkle with the garnish and drizzle with olive oil.

Store the dip in a sealed container in the fridge for up to 5 days.

MUHAMARA DIP

We can all become bored with serving the same dishes, so it's great to add another dip to your repertoire. This dip also makes a lovely relish on sandwiches as it works well with most roasted meats.

Makes about 500 ml (17 fl oz/2 cups)

4 red capsicums (peppers)
4 garlic cloves
60 g (2¼ oz) walnuts
60 g (2¼ oz) dry breadcrumbs
2 large fresh red chillies
3 tablespoons olive oil
3 tablespoons pomegranate molasses
juice of ½ lemon
1 teaspoon ground cumin
1 teaspoon ground coriander
1 teaspoon salt

Preheat the oven to 180°C (350°F).

Put the capsicums on a baking tray and roast for about 25–30 minutes, until they are quite coloured and almost charred. Using tongs, transfer the capsicums to a plastic bag. Wrap the plastic bag in a tea towel (dish towel) and set aside to cool for about 20 minutes.

When the capsicums are cool enough to handle, remove and discard the skin and seeds. Put the capsicum flesh, garlic, walnuts, breadcrumbs and red chillies in a food processer and blitz until the mixture forms a relatively smooth paste. Add the remaining ingredients and blitz until combined. Taste and season with a little more salt, if needed.

Store the dip in a sealed container in the fridge for up to 5 days.

TARAMASALATA

You can never have enough 'on arrival' dishes in your repertoire, and guests are always impressed by homemade taramasalata. You can also make this just to spoil yourself at home.

Makes 500 ml (17 fl oz/2 cups)

4 slices white bread, crusts removed
100 g (3½ oz) fish roe (red lumpfish caviar, trout roe, salmon roe or cod roe)
1 garlic clove, crushed
2 French shallots, finely chopped
juice of ½ lemon
250 ml (9 fl oz/1 cup) light olive oil
white pepper, to season

Rinse the bread slices under running water for just a few seconds. Firmly squeeze out the excess water.

Put the bread in a food processor with the fish roe, garlic and shallot and blend to a very smooth paste. Add the lemon juice and then, with the motor running, slowly pour in the olive oil. The mixture will thicken. Season with salt and white pepper.

Store the dip in a sealed container in the fridge for up to 5 days.

BABA GHANOUSH

Baba ghanoush translates from Arabic as 'pampered poppa' or, as I say, 'spoiled dad'. The name 'baba ghanoush' probably came from the fact that the men would chargrill the eggplants while barbecuing, and this dip would be a treat because they wouldn't often light the charcoal.

Makes about 300 ml (10½ fl oz)

2 eggplants (aubergines)
2 tomatoes, chopped
2 handfuls coriander (cilantro),
    leaves picked and chopped
1 handful flat-leaf (Italian) parsley,
    leaves picked and chopped
3 spring onions (scallions),
    white part and some of the
    green part, finely chopped
3 garlic cloves, crushed
juice of 2 lemons
3 tablespoons olive oil

Heat the barbecue to high and place the whole eggplants on the rack. Cook, turning, until the skins blister and burn and the centres are soft. Alternatively, place the eggplants on a naked flame on a gas cooktop and cook, turning with tongs, until blackened. Set aside to cool.

When the eggplants are cool enough to handle, peel off and discard the skin. Don't worry if there is still some black on the eggplant itself as that adds to the flavour. Finely chop the flesh and put it in a bowl.

Add the remaining ingredients to the chopped eggplant and mix until combined. Season with salt and freshly ground black pepper.

Store the dip in a sealed container in the fridge for up to 5 days.

TARATOR

Tarator is a versatile dip that originated in Macedonia, Turkey or Bulgaria. It can also be served as a condiment with grilled fish. There are plenty of versions of tarator. I prefer using yoghurt instead of tahini because it gives a lighter, more refreshing taste. The nuts add a lovely complexity of flavour.

Makes about 250 ml (9 fl oz/1 cup)

2 tablespoons pine nuts, lightly toasted
60 g (2¼ oz) walnuts, lightly toasted
150 g (5½ oz) Greek-style yoghurt
3 tablespoons olive oil
3 garlic cloves, crushed
1 tablespoon finely chopped dill
sea salt flakes, to season

Lightly crush the pine nuts using a mortar and pestle. Transfer to a bowl. Crush the walnuts using the mortar and pestle. Tip the walnuts into the bowl with the pine nuts.

Add the yoghurt, olive oil, garlic and dill. Mix to combine, then season with sea salt.

NOTE
Tarator is best served on the day it is made. It can be stored in the fridge for up to 5 days, but the nuts might become a little soft.

Clockwise from far left:

Tarator (page 41),
baba ghanoush (page 41),
taramasalata (page 40),
hazelnut dukkah (page 46),
za'atar (page 67),
pumpkin hummus (page 48),
muhamara dip (page 40)

HUMMUS

There are many different ways of making hummus and everyone thinks their version is best. Classic hummus recipes use a mortar and pestle to break down the chickpeas, which will give you a more grainy texture than the smooth version I like to make. I also like to add fresh lemon juice, as it gives a slightly acidic edge and makes a lighter colour. You can use tinned chickpeas but the result will not be as silky and smooth. If you are using tinned chickpeas, you will need 500 g (1 lb 2 oz) drained chickpeas. Bring them to the boil in plenty of water, add the baking powder and cook for a further 5 minutes.

150 g (5½ oz) dried chickpeas
¼ teaspoon baking powder
5 garlic cloves, peeled
400 g (14 oz) raw tahini
1 teaspoon salt
pinch of ground cumin
100 ml (3½ fl oz) lemon juice

In a large saucepan or bowl, soak the chickpeas in plenty of cold water (at least four times the quantity of the dried chickpeas) for at least 12 hours – overnight is good. Change the water at least twice during this time.

Drain the chickpeas and rinse well. Transfer to a large saucepan and cover with plenty of water (at least twice as much in volume as the chickpeas). Bring to the boil, then cover and cook over medium heat for 2 hours, topping up the water as necessary.

After 2 hours, if the chickpeas are soft, add the baking powder. If not, continue cooking until they soften.

Cook for a further hour, or until the chickpeas start to break down but are not mushy.

Meanwhile, put the peeled whole garlic cloves in a food processor (don't use a stick blender) with 200 ml (7 fl oz) of water and blend until very smooth. Tip into a sieve and keep the liquid, discarding the puréed garlic.

Drain the chickpeas. Put them in the food processor and blend to a smooth paste; this will take 7–10 minutes. Add the tahini, reserved garlic water, salt and cumin. Blend well, scraping down the side occasionally and adding more water if necessary. Transfer to a large bowl. Gently whisk in the lemon juice (you don't want to over-aerate the hummus and lose the dense consistency).

HAZELNUT DUKKAH

Traditional dukkah, which is the Vegemite of Egypt, is made with peanuts rather than hazelnuts, and is eaten with olive oil and bread for breakfast. I love using roasted hazelnuts for my dukkah because they are nuttier in flavour and the skins are a beautiful colour. You can use peanuts or any other type of nut instead of hazelnuts.

1¾ cups hazelnuts
1 tablespoon coriander seeds
1 tablespoon cumin seeds
1¼ cups sesame seeds
2 teaspoons sea salt flakes
2 teaspoons freshly ground
  black pepper

Preheat the oven to 160°C (315°F).

Put the hazelnuts on one baking tray, and the coriander and cumin seeds on a separate tray, and bake until toasted, approximately 15 minutes.

After the hazelnuts and seeds have been in the oven for 10 minutes, add the sesame seeds on a separate tray and toast for the remaining 5 minutes, or until lightly coloured. Remove all the trays from the oven and allow the nuts and seeds to cool to room temperature.

Put the hazelnuts in a food processor and pulse to a coarse breadcrumb size. (You could also crush the hazelnuts the traditional way using a mortar and pestle – good exercise for the biceps!) Transfer the hazelnuts to a large mixing bowl.

Put the cumin and coriander seeds in the food processor and process until almost a powder. (Use a mortar and pestle to do this if you prefer.)

Add this powder to the bowl along with the toasted sesame seeds, salt and pepper. Mix well using a wooden spoon.

Dukkah can be kept for up to a year – but I am sure you will eat it all before then! It is best stored in an airtight container in a cool, dry place.

LABNEH

A wonderful soft cheese, labneh is one of the easiest and most satisfying things you can make at home. You can use natural or Greek-style yoghurt for this recipe – the natural yoghurt will give a much silkier texture and less acidic flavour than the Greek-style yoghurt. I suggest you try this recipe with both and pick the one you like the most. I love eating labneh with lots of good-quality olive oil, a sprinkle of za'atar (see page 67) or hazelnut dukkah (see opposite), and some hot bread.

1 teaspoon salt
1 kg (2 lb 4 oz) natural or Greek-style
    yoghurt
juice of ½ lemon (if you are using
    natural yoghurt)

Mix the salt through the yoghurt. Hang a piece of muslin (cheesecloth) over a large bowl and pour the yoghurt into the cloth.

Hang the yoghurt in the fridge suspended over the bowl and allow the yoghurt to drain for 2–3 days; the longer you allow it to hang, the firmer the labneh will be.

Minimally drained, unrolled and unmarinated labneh will keep for 5–7 days. Marinated labneh will last for up to 2 weeks.

NOTE
Once the labneh is firm, you can add flavourings. Roll the labneh into tablespoon-size or larger balls and encrust them with chilli flakes, mild paprika, dried garlic, oregano, dried mint or whatever you like. Put the balls in a sterilised jar and top with olive oil, then store in the fridge. A beautifully wrapped jar of flavoured labneh balls is a great homemade gift.

PUMPKIN HUMMUS

Pumpkin hummus is a great take on the classic – it's easier to make and takes much less time and effort. Serve it as a dip when your guests arrive or as part of a shared table. It works equally well with fish and meat dishes.

Makes about 800 g (1 lb 12 oz)

700 g (1 lb 9 oz) butternut pumpkin (squash), peeled and cut into chunks
3 tablespoons olive oil
3 garlic cloves
white pepper, to season
200 g (7 oz) tahini
juice of 1–1½ lemons

Preheat the oven to 170°C (340°F). Line a baking tray with baking paper.

Put the pumpkin in a large bowl and toss with the olive oil and garlic cloves. Season with salt and white pepper. Spread over the baking tray and bake for 25–30 minutes, until the pumpkin is soft but not coloured.

When the pumpkin is cool enough to handle, transfer it to a food processor. Add 125 ml (4 fl oz/½ cup) of water and the tahini and lemon juice, to taste. Blitz until the mixture is smooth and well combined. Check the seasoning and add more salt and lemon juice, if needed.

Store the pumpkin hummus in a sealed container in the fridge for up to 5 days.

BEETROOT, CUMIN AND GOAT'S CURD DIP

A beautifully coloured dip with an earthy flavour that is balanced with the delicacy of the goat's curd.

Makes 550 g (1 lb 4 oz)

1 large beetroot (beet), trimmed
2 garlic cloves, peeled
1 teaspoon ground cumin
2½ tablespoons olive oil
200 g (7 oz/¾ cup) goat's curd

Put the whole beetroot in a medium saucepan and cover with cold water. Bring to the boil over medium–high heat and boil until tender, around 30–45 minutes, depending on the size of the beetroot.

Drain the beetroot and allow it to cool until you are able to handle it. Peel off the skin and cut the flesh into chunks.

Put the beetroot, garlic and cumin in a food processor and blitz until you have a smooth paste. Slowly drizzle in the olive oil, blitzing until everything is combined.

Transfer to a medium bowl, season with salt and freshly ground black pepper and fold in the goat's curd.

Store this dip in an airtight container in the fridge for up to 5 days.

GREEN OLIVES, WHITE ANCHOVIES AND CORIANDER SEEDS

Gourmet up your olives with this recipe. It's a perfect nibble when you have guests over, or you can serve it with grilled fish or steak. There is enough salt in the anchovies and olives to make it unnecessary to add more.

Serves 4 as a side dish

1 tablespoon coriander seeds
300 g (10½ oz) large green olives, pitted
1 handful coriander (cilantro), leaves
   finely chopped
4 tablespoons extra virgin olive oil,
   plus extra, to drizzle
50 g (1¾ oz) white anchovy fillets, in oil

Heat a frying pan over medium heat. Add the coriander seeds and dry-fry for 3 minutes, or until fragrant. Crush the seeds using a mortar and pestle.

Put the olives, coriander seeds, chopped coriander and olive oil in a large bowl and toss to combine. Scatter the anchovy fillets over the top and drizzle with olive oil.

GREEN TAHINI

My green tahini is a take on the classic tahini – which is whiter in colour – and is used as a dressing, a dip or a complement to hummus. The addition of more herbs in my version gives it a vibrant green colour, as well as a grassy flavour and fragrance that works well with many dishes.

Makes 200 g (7 oz)

2 cups coriander (cilantro), leaves
   coarsely chopped
125 ml (4 fl oz/½ cup) lemon juice
2 garlic cloves, peeled
90 g (3¼ oz/⅓ cup) tahini
1 teaspoon sea salt flakes

In a food processor, blend the coriander with 100 ml (3½ fl oz) water until you have a smooth green paste; don't overblend as the coriander will go black. Add the lemon juice, garlic and tahini and blend until smooth. Stir through the sea salt flakes.

Store this dip in an airtight container in the fridge for up to 5 days.

Clockwise from left:

*Beetroot, cumin and
goat's curd dip* (page 48),
hummus (page 44),
green tahini (page 49),
labneh (page 47),
toum (page 52)

GREEN ZHOUG

You can add this chilli paste to salads, have it with hummus, finish a stew with it or, as I love to do, add it to a risotto for a nice kick. Green zhoug has so many uses, and it will last for a few weeks in the fridge.

Makes 600 g (1 lb 5 oz)

15 large green chillies, chopped
10 garlic cloves, peeled
1 large handful coriander (cilantro),
    leaves and stems chopped
1 large handful flat-leaf (Italian)
    parsley, chopped
250 ml (9 fl oz/1 cup) olive oil

Put the chillies, garlic, coriander and parsley in a food processor and blend to a paste. Add the olive oil and salt to taste, and whiz to combine. Transfer to a sterilised jar and store in the fridge for up to 2 weeks.

TOUM

Definitely one for garlic lovers, toum is a traditional Middle Eastern dip that can also be served as a condiment with steak or chicken, or added as an extra seasoning to salad dressings. The quantity of garlic can be adjusted to taste.

Makes 200 g (7 oz)

12 garlic cloves, peeled
1 teaspoon sea salt flakes
250 ml (9 fl oz/1 cup) olive oil
juice of 2 lemons

Put the garlic and salt in a food processor and blitz to a smooth paste. Slowly drizzle in the olive oil while the motor is running. The mixture will thicken and is ready when it has the consistency of room-temperature butter.

Transfer to a mixing bowl and add the lemon juice to taste.

Toum will keep in an airtight container in the fridge for up to 2 weeks.

ROASTED BABY BEETROOT WITH LABNEH

The creamy texture of the labneh and the earthy flavour of the beetroot work extraordinarily well together. You can use this dish any way you like – as a dip, salad or vegetable accompaniment.

12–15 baby beetroot (beets), trimmed
   and washed thoroughly
5 thyme sprigs, plus 2 teaspoons
   thyme leaves
100 ml (3½ fl oz) olive oil,
   plus extra for drizzling
1 tablespoon coriander seeds,
   lightly toasted and crushed
3 tablespoons red wine vinegar
350 g (12 oz) labneh
1 handful oregano, leaves picked
100 g (3½ oz) natural almonds, lightly
   toasted and coarsely crushed

Preheat the oven to 180°C (350°F).

Tear off several sheets of foil. Put 4–5 beetroot on one sheet of foil, add a sprig of thyme and drizzle with a tablespoon of olive oil. Wrap with another sheet of foil to enclose the beetroot. Repeat until all the beetroot are wrapped and you have 3 foil parcels. Place the beetroot parcels on a baking tray and roast for 35–40 minutes, until a knife easily goes through the unwrapped beetroot. Remove the beetroot from the oven but do not unwrap them; allow to cool for 10 minutes.

Once the beetroot are cool enough to handle, peel off the skin and cut into halves or quarters. Add to a bowl with the coriander seeds, thyme leaves, red wine vinegar and 100 ml (3½ fl oz) of olive oil and mix to coat the beetroot. Season with salt and freshly ground black pepper. Set aside to marinate for 1 hour.

Spread the labneh over a large platter, top with the beetroot and sprinkle with the oregano leaves and crushed almonds. Season with salt and pepper and spoon the marinade over the top.

GREEN BEANS WITH GOAT'S CHEESE, ALMONDS AND LEMON

Kristy cooks dinner most Sunday nights as it's the end of a busy week of cooking for me. One of my favourite meals she cooks is barbecued steak with a few different vegetables, and this is one of her best recipes. The lemon zest and goat's cheese almost melt together to make the most delicious topping, taking the beans to a new level.

500 g (1 lb 2 oz) green beans,
 topped and tailed
grated zest of 1½ lemons
olive oil, for drizzling
100 g (3½ oz) marinated
 goat's cheese
50 g (1¾ oz) slivered almonds,
 lightly toasted

Blanch the beans in a saucepan of boiling water for 1–2 minutes, until done to your liking. Drain well and shake off any excess water.

Put the lemon zest and olive oil in a large bowl. Add the beans and toss to coat.

Transfer the hot beans to a serving dish and top with the goat's cheese and toasted almonds.

MUTABAL

To me, the difference between mutabal and baba ghanoush is that mutabal contains mainly eggplant and tahini, while baba ghanoush has different variations and ingredients such as tomatoes, onions and herbs, and it doesn't necessarily contain tahini. Ordinarily, I don't like smoky flavours, but I am drawn to this dish because the tahini gives it a nutty, creamy and delicate flavour and texture. It's great as a dip with drinks, as a condiment with meats or as part of a shared table. You can serve it drizzled with olive oil and sprinkled with pomegranate seeds and chopped herbs.

3 large eggplants (aubergines)
3 garlic cloves, crushed
120 g (4¼ oz) tahini
juice of 1 lemon
mint leaves, to garnish (optional)
pomegranate seeds, to garnish
   (optional)

Heat the barbecue to high and place the whole eggplants on the rack. Cook, turning, until the skins blister and burn. Alternatively, place the eggplants on a naked flame on a gas cooktop and cook, turning with tongs, until blackened. Set aside to cool.

When the eggplants are cool enough to handle, peel off and discard the skin. Put the eggplant flesh and garlic in a food processor and blitz until just combined. Add the tahini and lemon juice and blitz again, then season with salt.

Store the dip in a sealed container in the fridge for up to 5 days. To serve, garnish with mint leaves and pomegranate seeds (optional).

NOTES

Charring the eggplants on a barbecue or gas cooktop gives them a lovely smoky flavour. You can bake them in the oven, but they won't have the same flavour. Preheat the oven to 220°C (425°F) and cook the eggplants on a baking tray until charred.

If you are in a hurry, you can drop the charred eggplants into iced water to cool them down.

PIZZA DOUGH

Once you have mastered this recipe, it is very easy to make your own dough each time you feel like pizza and you will never want to order takeaway pizza again. This dough is best used within 2 hours of preparation and I don't recommend freezing it.

14 g (½ oz) dried yeast
1 tablespoon caster (superfine) sugar
500 ml (17 fl oz/2 cups) warm water
50 ml (1½ fl oz) olive oil
1 kg (2 lb 4 oz) 00 flour or plain
    (all-purpose) flour, plus extra
    for dusting
1 tablespoon salt

Using an electric mixer fitted with a hook attachment, mix the yeast, sugar and warm water until the yeast and sugar have dissolved. Reduce the speed to low and add the oil, then add the flour and mix until the dough comes together as a soft ball. This will take about 5 minutes. Add the salt and mix for a further 2–3 minutes (adding the salt last means it won't slow down the yeast). The dough should not be too firm or too wet.

Transfer the dough onto a lightly floured board. Divide the dough into 8 balls and put them on a large baking tray lined with baking paper. Wring out a wet tea towel (dish towel) and use it to cover the dough balls. Leave the dough balls to rise for 1 hour, or until they have doubled in size.

To shape the dough, lightly flour a dough ball all over. Holding the dough with both hands, work around the dough, carefully stretching it in a circular motion and taking care not to tear it. Shape the dough so that the centre is thinner than the crust.

ZUCCHINI AND ZA'ATAR EMPANADA

Zucchini is a completely underrated vegetable, and I use it in many different recipes as it is available all year round. If you are not a zucchini fan, use another vegetable to make the filling for this traditional South American pie.

DOUGH

500 g (1 lb 2 oz/3⅓ cups) plain
    (all-purpose) flour, plus extra
    for rolling
2 teaspoons sea salt flakes
    1 tablespoon sugar
250 g (9 oz) butter, at room
    temperature
250 g (9 oz) Greek-style yoghurt
1 egg, beaten

FILLING

5 small firm zucchini (courgettes)
    3 tablespoons olive oil
70 g (2½ oz) pine nuts, lightly toasted
150 g (5½ oz) Danish feta cheese,
    crumbled
1 handful za'atar or oregano leaves
grated zest of 1 lemon

To make the dough, put the flour, sea salt flakes and sugar in a food processor and blitz for a few seconds to combine. Add the butter and yoghurt and blitz until almost combined. Form the dough into a ball, wrap in plastic wrap and refrigerate for 2 hours.

While the dough is resting, make the filling. Cut the zucchini into 2–3 mm (1/16–1/8 inch) thick slices. Coat with the olive oil and season with salt and freshly ground black pepper. Heat a barbecue grill plate or chargrill pan to high. Cook the zucchini for 1 minute on each side (do not overcook it as it will cook further in the oven).

Transfer the zucchini to a bowl and gently fold in the pine nuts, feta, za'atar or oregano leaves and lemon zest. Taste and add extra seasoning if needed – be careful with the salt as the feta is salty and the zucchini has already been seasoned. Set aside to cool to room temperature.

Preheat the oven to 180°C (350°F). Line a large baking tray with baking paper.

Divide the dough in half and roll out on a lightly floured surface to make two circles, one about 24 cm (9½ inches) for the base and one about 28 cm (11¼ inches) for the top of the pie. The top will be slightly thinner than the base.

Put the smaller dough circle on the baking tray and mound the filling in the centre, leaving a 2 cm (¾ inch) border around the edge. Brush some beaten egg around the edge of the base. Place the larger dough circle on top and press the edge together using a fork to seal it. Score the top into wedges and cut a small hole in the centre of the dough to release the steam during cooking. Brush the top with beaten egg and bake for 25–30 minutes, until golden.

SCORCHED ONIONS WITH POMEGRANATE MOLASSES AND HALOUMI

Scorched onions are a childhood favourite of mine and they always remind me of a barbecue gathering. The pomegranate adds a lovely sweetness and acidity that makes this recipe work well as a side dish with any grilled meat or fish.

5 small red onions, halved crossways
3 tablespoons olive oil
2 tablespoons pomegranate molasses
50 g (1¾ oz) haloumi cheese

Preheat the oven to 180°C (350°F).

Heat a chargrill pan to high. Put the onion halves in a bowl and toss with the olive oil. Put the onions in the chargrill pan, cut side down, and cook for 4–5 minutes without turning, until grill marks appear. Turn the onions over and then transfer to the oven for 5 minutes to finish cooking.

Transfer the onions to a serving plate or platter and drizzle with the pomegranate molasses. Shave the haloumi over the top and serve.

FIGS WITH BURRATA AND PROSCIUTTO

This dish is all about celebrating simplicity and letting the flavours of these special ingredients shine. I prefer pomegranate molasses to caramelised balsamic vinegar, as it is less acidic and it adds a complex yet harmonious flavour. Use a large, flat serving platter to assemble and serve the dish.

4 x 100 g (3½ oz) or 2 x 200 g (7 oz) burrata cheese balls, drained
6 fresh figs, halved lengthways
100 g (3½ oz) sliced prosciutto
3 tablespoons pomegranate molasses
100 ml (3½ fl oz) olive oil
10 basil leaves
black salt, to serve

Place the burrata balls on a large serving platter. Add the fig halves and the prosciutto, arranging the ingredients in an uneven way.

Drizzle the pomegranate molasses and olive oil over the top. Sprinkle with the basil leaves, black salt and freshly cracked black pepper.

PITA BREAD

The basic bread eaten all around the Middle East, pita bread is delicious with hummus and can be filled with just about anything you like. The dough can be used in many other recipes and cut to whatever size or shape you like.

500 g (1 lb 2 oz/3⅓ cups) strong bread
   flour, sifted, plus extra for dusting
1 x 7 g (¼ oz) dry yeast sachet
1 tablespoon sea salt flakes
2½ tablespoons extra virgin olive oil
350 ml (12 fl oz) warm water

Put the flour, yeast and salt in a large bowl and mix to combine. Make a well in the centre and slowly add the olive oil. Using your hands, combine the flour and oil. Gradually add enough warm water to make a slightly sticky dough (you may not need to use all of it). The dough will come together when you start kneading it.

Dust a work surface with flour and knead the dough for 3–4 minutes, until it forms a nice smooth consistency.

Put the dough in a clean bowl and cover with a damp tea towel (dish towel) or plastic wrap with a few holes pricked in it. Leave in a warm place to rise for 1 hour, or until doubled in size.

Cut the dough into 8 equal pieces. Roll each piece of dough into a ball (or whatever shape you like). Dust the work surface with extra flour, place the 8 balls of dough on it and cover with the damp tea towel or plastic wrap with holes to rise again for 30 minutes.

Roll out each ball of dough into a circle about 5 mm (¼ inch) thick, or whatever thickness you like. Leave to rest for 20 minutes.

Preheat the oven to 180°C (350°F). Line a baking tray with baking paper or preheat a pizza stone (they give the bread a nice colour).

Put the dough circles on the baking tray or pizza stone (you may need to cook them in batches) and bake for 10–15 minutes, or until light golden. Cool on a tea towel so the pita breads do not lose too much moisture. Use within 1–2 days. These pita breads can also be frozen, as soon as they have been cooled, for up to 3 weeks.

ZA'ATAR BREAD

When I was a kid, there was a bakery close to our house and on the weekends we used to go there for fresh pita and za'atar bread. But by the time we got home, we would have eaten most of it – I mean, who can resist freshly baked bread? The smell of this bread cooking is the true smell of the Middle East.

1 quantity pita bread dough
 (see page 65)
½ cup za'atar (see below)
150 ml (5 fl oz) good-quality olive oil

Make the dough according to the instructions on page 65. Once you've rolled the balls of dough into rounds and set them aside to rest for 20 minutes, preheat the oven to 180°C (350°F) and line a baking tray with baking paper.

Put the za'atar and olive oil in a bowl. Mix to combine.

Gently press your fingers into the dough rounds, making little valleys just deep enough so the za'atar oil won't roll off the dough. (Don't press too hard as you want the dough to remain aerated.) Spoon the za'atar oil over the dough.

Put the dough circles on the baking tray (you may need to cook them in batches) and bake for 10–15 minutes, or until light golden. Cool on a tea towel (dish towel) and use within 1–2 days.

ZA'ATAR

Za'atar leaf is available only seasonally and not always easy to find – a specialised Middle Eastern grocery store may stock it. This recipe provides an excellent alternative and makes 40 g (1½ oz) za'atar mixture.

Preheat the oven to 50°C (120°F) or the lowest setting. Dry 2 handfuls thyme leaves by spreading the thyme sprigs over a baking tray and letting them dry out in the oven for 1 hour or more if necessary. When cool enough to handle, gently break off the leaves. Alternatively, you can spread the thyme sprigs out on a tea towel (dish towel) and dry them outside in the sun.

Combine the dried thyme with 2 tablespoons ground sumac, 2 teaspoons sea salt flakes and 2 tablespoons toasted sesame seeds. Transfer to an airtight container and store in a cool, dark place for up to a month.

GRILLED SARDINES WITH HARISSA

Whether you cook them on a barbecue or in the oven, you'll love these sardines wrapped in vine leaves. You can buy pickled vine leaves from Middle Eastern grocery stores, and fresh ones at farmers' markets, or you may have a friend who has a grapevine at home. If you are using fresh vine leaves, you'll need to blanch them in boiling salted water for 2–3 minutes, or until they change colour. Refresh in icy cold water and pat dry with paper towel.

16 sardines
6 teaspoons red harissa (see below), plus extra, to serve
16 large or 32 small vine leaves
3 tablespoons olive oil
lemon wedges, to serve

Cut a slit in the belly of the sardines, or ask your fishmonger to do this for you. Rinse in cold water and pat dry. Rub the sardines with the harissa, inside and out.

Depending on the size of the vine leaf you are using, lay 1 or 2 leaves on a work surface, place a sardine on the diagonal and wrap. It is okay if the head and tail are poking out at either end. Rub the vine leaf parcels with the olive oil and season with salt and freshly ground black pepper.

Heat the barbecue to medium–high and cook the vine-wrapped sardines for 2–3 minutes on each side. Alternatively, you can cook them on a baking tray for 8–10 minutes in an oven preheated to 180°C (350°F). If cooking in the oven, you will not need to turn them.

Serve with lemon wedges and extra red harissa on the side.

RED HARISSA
Put 700 g (1 lb 9 oz) roasted capsicums (peppers), 6 peeled garlic cloves, 2 large green chillies and 2 handfuls washed and chopped coriander (cilantro) leaves and stems in a food processor, and blend to a paste. Add 3 teaspoons mild paprika, 2 teaspoons ground cumin, 2 teaspoons ground coriander and 2 teaspoons caster (superfine) sugar, and blend for a further minute. Add 2½ tablespoons red wine vinegar and salt to taste, then drizzle in 200 ml (7 fl oz) extra virgin olive oil slowly with the motor running until combined. Store in an airtight container in the fridge for up to 2 weeks.

Makes 20 small balls

SHANKLISH CHEESE WITH ZA'ATAR

These versatile yoghurt cheese balls make a great snack or an accompaniment to a shared table. You can also use them to make a salad by flaking the balls and mixing them with fresh tomatoes and olive oil, or you could use them in a pasta dish.

1 kg (2 lb 4 oz) Greek-style yoghurt
1 tablespoon sweet paprika
1 small fresh red chilli, chopped
    and crushed
100 g (3½ oz) za'atar spice mix
    (page 67)

Put the yoghurt and 200 ml (7 fl oz) of water in a saucepan and whisk to combine. Bring to a gentle simmer over medium–low heat, mixing once or twice until the mixture separates into curds and whey.

Line a colander with a large piece of muslin (cheesecloth) and pour in the yoghurt mixture. Drain over the sink until the mixture is firm, dry and cool. This will take about 2 hours.

Meanwhile, combine the remaining ingredients in a shallow bowl.

Transfer the firm yoghurt to a bowl. Season with salt and gently mix to combine. Using clean hands, shape the mixture into 20 even balls, then roll them in the za'atar mixture.

Traditionally these are kept in an airtight glass jar and covered completely with olive oil. They will keep like this in the fridge for around 2–3 months, but you can also store them without the oil in an airtight container in the fridge for up to 3 weeks.

NOTE
Za'atar spice mix, available in Middle Eastern grocery stores, contains dried za'atar leaves, sesame seeds, ground sumac and other spices. To make your own, see the recipe on page 67.

YEMENITE PAN ROTI

Great served with stews, these roti are also delicious for breakfast with chopped tomato, chilli and hard-boiled eggs. The dough needs to be rested overnight, so this recipe is made over 2 days.

500 g (1 lb 2 oz/3⅓ cups) plain (all-purpose) flour, sifted, plus extra for dusting
20 g (¾ oz) dark brown sugar
1 teaspoon salt
200 g (7 oz) butter, melted and cooled, plus extra melted butter for greasing
oil spray for greasing
olive oil or clarified butter, for cooking

Put the flour, sugar and salt in a bowl and mix to combine. Slowly add 400 ml (14 fl oz) water and mix until you have a soft but not too sticky dough (you may not need all the water).

Dust a work surface lightly with flour and knead the dough for 5 minutes, or until you have a smooth ball. Alternatively, you can mix the dough using an electric stand mixer with a dough hook for 2–3 minutes (do not overmix). Wrap the dough in plastic wrap and let it rest in the fridge for at least 2 hours.

Divide the dough into 8 equal balls. Using your hands, spread some of the melted butter onto a work surface. Coat your palms with more melted butter. Working with one dough ball at a time, stretch the dough as thinly as possible into a rectangle, then brush melted butter over the dough.

Fold the long edges of the stretched dough into the centre, then fold the shorter edges into the centre. You should have a small rectangle. Repeat this process at least three times. (You are creating layers as you would in puff pastry.) Repeat with the remaining balls of dough.

Spray a baking tray with oil. Put the dough rectangles on the tray, cover with plastic wrap and let the dough rest overnight in the fridge.

When ready to cook the roti, grease the work surface with melted butter. Stretch out each piece of dough to approximately 20 cm (8 inches) in diameter on the greased surface.

Heat a frying pan with a lid to medium-low heat. Add 1 teaspoon olive oil or clarified butter to the pan and add a piece of the stretched dough. Put the lid on the pan and cook until lightly golden, approximately 4–5 minutes each side. Repeat with the remaining dough.

These roti are best eaten on the day they are cooked, but can be made in advance and warmed just before serving.

PICKLED LEBANESE-STYLE BABY EGGPLANTS

I was introduced to these pickles by a Lebanese friend of mine. His mother used to make them for him here in Australia. I was intrigued by their amazing, intense flavour. These eggplants are an excellent addition to your mezze table.

1 kg (2 lb 4 oz) baby eggplants (aubergines), preferably purple, not green
100 g (3½ oz) walnuts
6 garlic cloves, crushed
2 tablespoons rock salt
3 tablespoons pomegranate molasses
1 handful coriander (cilantro), leaves and stems finely chopped
1 tablespoon chilli flakes
1 tablespoon sweet paprika
3 tablespoons red wine vinegar
250 ml (9 fl oz/1 cup) olive oil, approximately

Cut off and discard the eggplant tops. Thoroughly wash the eggplants, then put them in a large saucepan and cover with cold water. Cover the eggplants with a plate to keep them submerged. Bring to the boil, then cook over medium heat for 15 minutes. Drain and allow to cool to room temperature.

Cover a baking tray with a tea towel (dish towel). Cut a slit in the side of each eggplant, open it out flat and place it on the tray. Put another tea towel on top and press down with a weight. Set the eggplants aside overnight, or for at least 8 hours. This will remove any excess water.

Chop the walnuts until they are roughly the size of grains of rice. Mix with the garlic, salt, pomegranate molasses, coriander and chilli flakes. Stuff the mixture into the slits in the eggplants. Put a layer of eggplants in the bottom of a sterilised jar and sprinkle with some paprika. Add the remaining eggplants in layers, sprinkling with more paprika and adding 1 tablespoon of the red wine vinegar after every layer of eggplants. Pour in enough of the olive oil to fill the jar and seal. Place the jar in a dark place (the back of a cupboard is ideal) for 3 weeks.

After 3 weeks, the pickled eggplants are ready to eat. Once opened, store in the fridge for up to 2 weeks.

LAMB PIZZA

Nothing speaks of my childhood more than this Middle Eastern style pizza, 'bil ajin' (dough and meat). Junk food and fast-food chains were just beginning to appear in Tel Aviv when I was growing up. Of course, being kids we wanted to try all the new food, but my mum was still a bit old-fashioned and insisted on cooking every day. Instead of takeaways, she would create recipes that were Middle Eastern interpretations of Western food – that was her way of selling it to us. It always worked. Thanks, Mum!

3 tablespoons olive oil, plus extra
 for drizzling
1 brown onion, finely chopped
600 g (1 lb 5 oz) minced (ground) lamb
3 tablespoons chermoula (page 125)
½ quantity pizza dough (page 58)
plain (all-purpose) flour, for dusting
Greek-style yoghurt or labneh, to serve
toasted pine nuts, to serve
mint leaves, to garnish

Preheat the oven to 250°C (500°F). Place a pizza stone or baking tray in the oven to heat up at least 1 hour prior to cooking the pizza.

Heat the oil in a frying pan over medium heat and sauté the onion for 3–5 minutes. Increase the heat to high, add the lamb and cook, stirring and breaking up the lumps, for 5 minutes. Stir the chermoula through the lamb and cook for 1 minute, without cooking the lamb all the way through.

Divide the pizza dough into quarters and roll each into a ball. Lightly flour one dough ball all over. Holding the dough with both hands, work around the dough, carefully stretching it in a circular motion and taking care not to tear it. Shape the dough so that the centre is thinner than the crust.

Spread a quarter of the lamb mixture over the pizza base. Carefully put the pizza onto the hot pizza stone or baking tray and bake for 3–5 minutes, until the edge of the pizza is coloured and the base is cooked. Transfer the cooked pizza to a plate. Repeat with the remaining dough and lamb mixture.

Drizzle each pizza with some good-quality olive oil and top with a few dollops of Greek-style yoghurt or labneh, some toasted pine nuts and mint leaves.

NOTES

For best results, use a pizza stone. If you don't have a pizza stone, you can use a baking tray. I suggest assembling each pizza just before you put it in the oven, rather than preparing all four at once and leaving them to sit while the others are cooking.

BEETROOT-PICKLED CUCUMBERS

Pickles are an essential condiment that are always included on the table in any Middle Eastern home. It is not considered a meal if there aren't any pickles!

1 kg (2 lb 4 oz) baby (or smallest you can find) Lebanese (short) cucumbers

310 ml (10¾ fl oz/1¼ cups) red wine vinegar

½ cup (150 g) salt

1 tablespoon caster (superfine) sugar

1 large beetroot (beet), washed and trimmed

4 garlic cloves, peeled

1 handful dill, including stems, washed and drained

Wash the cucumbers well and set on a clean tea towel (dish towel) to dry.

Mix 1.5 litres (52 fl oz/6 cups) water with the vinegar, salt and sugar until the salt and sugar dissolve. This mixture should taste salty like sea water.

Cut the beetroot into chunks (the smaller the chunks, the more colour you will have in the cucumbers) and layer them in a sterilised 2 litre (70 fl oz/8 cup) jar with the whole cucumbers, garlic and dill. Pour the liquid over, seal and set aside for a week.

These pickled cucumbers can be stored in the sealed sterilised jar for up to 2 months. If keeping them for longer, it is best to pour a little olive oil on the top of the water.

DATES STUFFED WITH GOAT'S CHEESE AND PISTACHIOS

When you run out of time and still want an impressive dessert, this is definitely a winner. It doesn't require much effort and there is zero cooking time. You could leave out the sugar and honey and serve this as a savoury dish when guests arrive. It's also a lovely addition to a cheese board.

200 g (7 oz) goat's cheese,
  at room temperature

4 tablespoons milk

1 tablespoon sugar

20 medjool dates, scored down the centre
  and pitted

4 tablespoons pistachio nuts,
  lightly toasted and crushed

4 tablespoons honey

Put the goat's cheese, milk and sugar in a bowl and mix with a spoon to soften the goat's cheese. Spoon the mixture into a piping (icing) bag and use it to fill the dates.

Arrange the stuffed dates on a serving plate. Scatter the pistachios over the top and drizzle with the honey.

Salads

Our recipes have always featured plenty of vegetables, as they are so affordable and accessible, and delicious when prepared in the right way. Animals in the Middle East are often kept in the family garden to provide milk and eggs – not meat – and the emphasis is very much on homegrown vegetables. We believe that a salad should be something that is thoughtfully put together. The salads here feature simple ingredients and can be eaten as side dishes with your main course, or as meals on their own. They make excellent lunches.

BURRATA, RADISH AND CHIVE SALAD

I like to use a lot of different vegetables as bases for my salads – just not all at the same time. I choose one or two things that are beautiful at that moment, then pair them with other ingredients or spices that help to show them off. Here, peppery radishes balance the creaminess of the burrata cheese. It's a light summery dish that could easily be doubled or even tripled for a shared table and served with a warm loaf of crusty bread.

150 g (5½ oz) sugar snap peas, trimmed
3 x 100 g (3½ oz) burrata cheese
    balls, drained
sea salt
4 tablespoons extra virgin olive oil
juice of 2 lemons
100 g (3½ oz/1 bunch) small radishes,
    very thinly sliced
30 g (1 oz) chives, cut into 3 cm
    (1¼ inch) lengths

Blanch the sugar snap peas in a saucepan of boiling water, then drain and plunge them into a bowl of iced water to cool.

Tear the burrata into a large serving bowl – the cream will ooze out into the bowl and form part of the dressing. Spread the burrata around the bowl. Scatter half the sugar snap peas over the burrata. Season with sea salt, half the olive oil and half the lemon juice. Add the radishes, the remaining sugar snap peas and the chives.

Drizzle the remaining oil and lemon juice over the salad and season with sea salt and cracked black pepper.

NOTE
This salad is made in the bowl that you are going to serve it in. I suggest using a large, flat salad bowl with a rim.

Serves 8 as a side dish

WHITE BEAN AND SUMAC SALAD

To me, a salad should venture beyond cold chopped vegetables. It should have different textures and contrasting flavours and include something special that makes you want to go back for another helping. This is a light and refreshing dish that goes well with meat or fish. The lemon juice and sumac give it a lovely zing.

195 g (7 oz/1 cup) dried cannellini beans
1 large red onion, thinly sliced
1 large handful parsley, leaves
     coarsely chopped
1 large handful coriander (cilantro),
     leaves coarsely chopped
1½ large fresh red chillies, thinly sliced
3 tablespoons sumac
125 ml (4 fl oz/½ cup) olive oil
juice of 1 lemon

Put the dried beans in a large bowl and cover with 1.25 litres (44 fl oz/ 5 cups) water. Leave to soak for at least 12 hours, but ideally overnight.

Drain the beans and lightly rinse under cold running water. Transfer to a large saucepan with plenty of cold water and cook over medium–low heat for 1½ hours, or until the beans are tender but not mushy.

Drain and allow to cool completely.

Transfer the cooled beans to a large bowl and add the remaining ingredients. Season with salt and freshly ground black pepper and gently mix until combined, trying not to break up the beans.

NOTE
You can substitute two 400 g (14 oz) tins of cannellini beans for the dried beans. Simply drain them and mix with the other salad ingredients.

BROAD BEAN, TOMATO AND CUMIN SEED SALAD

If you want to know how sunshine tastes and looks on a plate, this is it. Serve this salad with anything and enjoy the way it instantly makes you feel healthy and happy.

500 g (1 lb 2 oz) broad beans, podded

200 g (7 oz) mixed heirloom cherry tomatoes, halved

1 large green chilli, seeds removed, finely diced

1 handful coriander (cilantro), leaves chopped

1 teaspoon cumin seeds, toasted and crushed

1 preserved lemon, skin only, chopped

3–4 spring onions (scallions), chopped

juice of 1 lemon

2½ tablespoons olive oil

Blanch the broad beans by putting them in boiling water for 1–2 minutes. Drain and cool under cold running water, then slip off the skins.

Put the peeled broad beans in a large bowl and add the remaining ingredients. Mix gently to combine.

NOTE

If making this salad in advance, prepare and combine all of the ingredients except the lemon juice and olive oil. Cover and refrigerate, adding the dressing ingredients when you are ready to serve.

DUKKAH EGG SALAD

Egg salad made with mayonnaise is a classic, but this version is a much more interesting alternative. There's a nice spicy kick from the chillies and a great acidity from the gherkins. It works really well as a breakfast dish or as part of a brunch, and is delicious on rye bread.

8 soft-boiled eggs
100 g (3½ oz) dukkah
15 g (½ oz/½ cup) dill, stems removed
50 g (1¾ oz) pickled chillies,
    coarsely chopped
100 g (3½ oz) gherkins (pickles),
    coarsely chopped
100 ml (3½ fl oz) olive oil

Peel the eggs and break them into about four chunks each. Add them to a bowl with the remaining ingredients and gently fold to combine.

NOTE
Use pickled jalapeño chillies if you can find them.

Serves 4 as a side dish

TABOULEH

Although this herb salad is a well-known basic in Mediterranean cuisine, I like to make a naughty version with chopped fried eggplant added for an extra flavour dimension.

1 tablespoon burghul (bulgur)
4 large handfuls flat-leaf (Italian)
    parsley, leaves finely chopped
1 handful mint, leaves finely chopped
4 spring onions (scallions), chopped
2 tomatoes, seeds removed, chopped
1 Lebanese (short) cucumber, chopped
4 tablespoons olive oil
4 tablespoons lemon juice
pomegranate seeds, to garnish

Soak the burghul in hot water for 1 minute. Drain and squeeze out any remaining liquid. Transfer to a large bowl and set aside to cool.

Add the parsley, mint, spring onion, tomato and cucumber to the bowl with the burghul. Stir gently to combine. Stir in the olive oil and lemon juice, and season with salt and freshly ground black pepper to taste. Scatter with pomegranate seeds to serve.

TZATZIKI SALAD

I've taken a recipe that's normally a dip and turned it into a salad. It's a lovely refreshing dish that works well with roasted lamb. You could toss some shredded chicken or fish through the salad for a main meal.

5 Lebanese (short) cucumbers
1 large fresh green chilli, sliced
1 large handful mint leaves,
    roughly torn
1 bunch watercress, leaves picked

DRESSING
250 g (9 oz) Greek-style yoghurt
1 garlic clove, crushed
2 teaspoons dried mint
50 ml (1½ fl oz) olive oil

Cut the cucumbers in half lengthways. Scoop out and discard some of the seeds. Cut the cucumbers into batons.

Put the cucumber in a large bowl with the chilli, mint and watercress, and mix with your hands to combine.

To make the dressing, put the yoghurt, garlic, mint and oil in a bowl and mix together. Season with salt and freshly ground black pepper.

Toss the dressing through the salad. Taste and add extra seasoning if needed.

Clockwise from top left:

Roasted baby beetroot with labneh (page 53),
white bean and sumac salad (page 86),
tzatziki salad (page 91),
zucchini and za'atar empanada (page 59)

TUNISIAN TUNA SALAD

*The 'sabich' or 'sabih' is a classic Middle Eastern
sandwich that happens to have all the textures needed
for a delicious salad. It has become one of my favourite
salads to make because it doesn't require too much
effort, as everything can be prepared in advance.
Although you can use tinned tuna, if you have the time
I suggest preserving your own tuna as it isn't difficult
and the results are very rewarding.*

200 g (7 oz) kipfler (fingerling) potatoes

50 g (1¾ oz) pitted black olives

2 tomatoes, cut into wedges

1 Lebanese (short) cucumber, chopped

3 tablespoons coarsely
   chopped coriander (cilantro), plus
   a few sprigs for garnish

3 soft-boiled eggs

250 g (9 oz) tinned tuna

DRESSING

2 tablespoons red harissa (page 68)

3 tablespoons olive oil

3 tablespoons red wine vinegar

Cook the potatoes in a large saucepan of boiling water until
tender. Drain and cool, then peel and cut into chunks.

Combine the potato chunks, olives, tomato, cucumber and
coriander in a large bowl and mix together.

To make the dressing, combine the harissa, oil and vinegar
in a bowl. Season with salt and freshly ground black pepper
and mix together until combined.

Carefully break open the eggs and arrange them on top of
the salad. Break the tuna into pieces and add it to the salad.
Drizzle the dressing over the top, season with black pepper
and serve garnished with a few sprigs of coriander.

Serves 4 as a starter

FIG, HALOUMI AND FRESH ZA'ATAR LEAVES

The combination of sweet and salty is intriguing and addictive. This salad is the Mediterranean equivalent of salted caramel in a savoury version and I can't get enough of it. It's very simple, quick and easy to make, but also elegant and impressive and a great starter when entertaining.

125 ml (4 fl oz/½ cup) light olive oil

500 g (1 lb 2 oz) haloumi cheese, cut into 8 slices

235 g (8½ oz/⅔ cup) honey

4 figs, halved lengthways

6 g (⅛ oz/½ cup) za'atar leaves or oregano leaves

100 g (3½ oz) walnuts, lightly toasted

Heat the oil in a large frying pan over medium heat. Add the haloumi and cook for 2 minutes on each side, or until golden brown.

Remove any excess oil from the pan, leaving the haloumi in the pan, and add the honey. Increase the heat to high and allow the honey to reduce slightly. It will become sticky and glossy. Add the figs and cook until warmed through.

Arrange the haloumi and figs on a platter, scatter with the za'atar or oregano and the walnuts and spoon over the warm honey.

WARM MOROCCAN CARROT SALAD

A friend of mine used to make this salad as a side dish for dinner every Friday night, and I felt the need to have it on my restaurant's menu too. I've added goat's cheese to give it an elegant edge.

800 g (1 lb 12 oz) baby carrots, trimmed and peeled

2 tablespoons olive oil

1 large green chilli, seeds removed, finely chopped

2 garlic cloves, crushed

1 tablespoon honey

1 teaspoon ground cumin

1 teaspoon sumac

50 g (1¾ oz) soft goat's cheese, crumbled

1 tablespoon finely chopped flat-leaf (Italian) parsley

extra virgin olive oil, to drizzle

Bring a medium saucepan filled with salted water to the boil. Add the carrots and boil for 3 minutes. Drain well.

Heat the olive oil in a large frying pan over medium heat. Add the carrots and cook for 1 minute, or until coated in oil. Add the chilli and garlic and cook for 1 minute, or until fragrant (but not coloured). Add the honey and cook for 1 minute, or until warmed through. Add the cumin and sumac, season to taste and toss well to combine. Remove the pan from the heat and allow the carrots to cool slightly then transfer to a serving plate.

Scatter the goat's cheese and parsley over the carrots and drizzle with extra virgin olive oil.

CAULIFLOWER AND CRANBERRY SALAD

You will need the seeds from a pomegranate for this salad, but any pomegranate juice that remains can be used to make a pomegranate mojito mocktail (see recipe below).

---

200 g (7 oz/1 cup) pearl barley
½ cauliflower, cut into small florets
1 pomegranate, seeds removed and reserved
75 g (2½ oz/½ cup) dried cranberries
60 g (2¼ oz/½ cup) chopped walnuts, toasted
75 g (2½ oz) chopped pistachio nut kernels
2 large handfuls flat-leaf (Italian) parsley, leaves chopped
4 mint sprigs, leaves chopped
3 tablespoons olive oil
3 tablespoons white balsamic or white wine vinegar
2 tablespoons pomegranate molasses

Put the pearl barley in a large saucepan of cold water. Bring to the boil over high heat. Reduce the heat to medium and cook for 40 minutes, or until tender. Drain, refresh in cold water and drain again.

Bring a medium saucepan of water to the boil with a pinch of salt. Blanch the cauliflower for 1 minute. Drain, refresh in cold water and drain again.

Put the pearl barley, cauliflower, pomegranate seeds, cranberries, walnuts, pistachios, parsley and mint in a large bowl. Toss to combine.

Put the olive oil, vinegar and pomegranate molasses in a small bowl. Whisk to combine, season to taste and pour over the cauliflower salad. Mix together gently and serve.

POMEGRANATE MOJITO MOCKTAIL
Put 2 lime quarters, 2 teaspoons pomegranate seeds, ¾ tablespoon sugar syrup and a sprig of mint leaves into each of four glasses. Gently mash the mixture with a muddling stick. (The mint leaves should be bruised to release the essential oils but not shredded.) Add 30 ml (1 fl oz) pomegranate juice to each glass and stir to dissolve the sugar and lift the mint up from the bottom of the glasses. Top each glass with crushed ice and 100 ml (3½ fl oz) soda water. Garnish with extra mint leaves and pomegranate seeds.

CLAUDIA'S CHOPPED VEGETABLE SALAD

This clean, light salad is one of the most basic in Israeli cuisine, and it can become a meal in itself when you add a protein such as tuna or chicken.

3 large truss tomatoes, diced
2 Lebanese (short) cucumbers, diced
1 small red onion, diced
4 radishes, diced
1 handful mint, leaves chopped
2 large handfuls flat-leaf (Italian) parsley, finely chopped
3–4 spring onions (scallions), finely chopped
juice of 1 lemon
125 ml (4 fl oz/½ cup) extra virgin olive oil

Put all of the ingredients in a large bowl, season with salt and freshly ground black pepper, and mix until combined.

If you are making this salad ahead of time, omit the lemon juice, oil and salt and pepper until you are ready to serve it.

NOTE
This salad is also delicious served with a yoghurt dressing, made by combining 250 g (9 oz) Greek-style yoghurt, 15 g (½ oz/¼ cup) chopped mint leaves, 4 crushed garlic cloves and 2 tablespoons olive oil.

TOM'S FENNEL SALAD

Tom, Kristy's younger brother, is a great cook. He made this salad for us many years ago when we visited him in Melbourne and we just loved the combination of the crisp fennel and the creamy feta. It has become a favourite salad in our house as well.

2 fennel bulbs, thinly shaved using a mandolin

2 Lebanese (short) cucumbers, thinly shaved lengthways using a mandolin

1 handful dill, coarsely chopped

2 large handfuls flat-leaf (Italian) parsley, coarsely chopped

1 handful mint leaves

100 g (3½ oz) feta cheese, crumbled

juice of 2 lemons

3 tablespoons extra virgin olive oil

50 g (1¾ oz/⅓ cup) pine nuts, toasted

Put the fennel, cucumber, dill, parsley and mint in a large bowl and toss gently to combine. Add the feta cheese and gently toss through using your hands.

Put the lemon juice and olive oil in a small bowl and whisk to combine. Pour the dressing over the salad, season with salt (with care, as the feta is quite salty) and gently mix through using your hands. Scatter the pine nuts over the top.

●

NOTE

If you are serving this salad with meat, use 1½ tablespoons white balsamic vinegar instead of the lemon juice.

HOT-SMOKED SALMON AND POTATO SALAD

Based on the classic Egyptian breakfast dish of dukkah and eggs, this salad is one of the most popular at Kepos Street Kitchen.

400 g (14 oz) kipfler potatoes, peeled, boiled and chopped

500 g (1 lb 2 oz) hot-smoked salmon (available from fish markets or vacuum-packed at supermarkets), flaked

12 Sicilian olives, pitted and chopped

4 eggs, soft-boiled

3 tablespoons extra virgin olive oil

4 tablespoons hazelnut dukkah (see page 46) or za'atar (see page 67)

1 handful flat-leaf (Italian) parsley, chopped

juice of 1 lemon

zest of ½ lemon

Put the potato, half of the salmon and the olives in a large bowl and mix gently. Tear apart 2 of the eggs and toss through the salad.

Put the olive oil, dukkah, parsley, lemon juice and zest in a bowl and whisk to combine. Pour over the salad and mix gently until combined.

To serve, tear apart the remaining 2 eggs and scatter over the salad with the remaining salmon.

Serves 4 as a side dish

BRUSSELS SPROUTS, POMEGRANATE AND SOFT FETA SALAD

Perhaps it's because I wasn't forced to eat them as a child that I love brussels sprouts now. I hope this recipe helps make people who have had a bad experience eating brussels sprouts in the past change their opinion.

100 g (3½ oz) Danish feta

2 tablespoons full-cream (whole) milk

500 g (1 lb 2 oz) brussels sprouts, trimmed and halved

1½ tablespoons olive oil

5 tablespoons pomegranate molasses

2 tablespoons chopped flat-leaf (Italian) parsley

1 small handful mint leaves

60 g (2¼ oz) pistachio nut kernels, coarsely chopped

½ pomegranate, seeds removed and reserved

extra virgin olive oil, to drizzle

Put the feta and milk in a food processor and blend until smooth. Transfer to a bowl and set aside in the fridge until ready to use.

Bring a medium saucepan of water to the boil with a pinch of salt. Blanch the brussels sprouts for 30 seconds then drain well.

Heat the olive oil in a medium frying pan over medium heat. Add the brussels sprouts and cook for 3–5 minutes, turning them as little as possible to get a chargrilled effect. Add the pomegranate molasses and cook until the brussels sprouts are caramelised, which should take 3–5 minutes. Remove from the heat.

Put the brussels sprouts in a bowl and season with salt. Add the parsley and mint and mix well. Scatter over the pistachios and pomegranate seeds, and add dollops of the feta mixture. Drizzle with olive oil and serve.

Serves 6–8 as a side dish

CAULIFLOWER, RAW TAHINI AND ZHOUG SALAD

The cauliflower is delicious deep-fried in this dish, but if you'd prefer a healthier version it can be roasted in the oven at 180°C/350°F for about 25 minutes instead.

rice bran oil, for deep-frying
1 large cauliflower, cut into large florets
sea salt flakes, to season
50 g (1¾ oz) raw tahini
juice of 1 lemon
olive oil, to drizzle
1 large handful coriander (cilantro), leaves finely chopped
1 tablespoon cumin seeds, toasted and crushed
2 tablespoons green zhoug (see page 52) or 1 large green chilli, finely chopped

Put enough rice bran oil in a large saucepan over high heat to cover and deep-fry the cauliflower. Heat the oil to 170°C (325°F), or until a cube of bread dropped into the oil turns golden brown in 20 seconds. Working in batches, deep-fry the cauliflower until golden, then drain on paper towel.

When ready to serve, put the cauliflower in a bowl and season with sea salt flakes. Combine the tahini, lemon juice and olive oil in a small bowl and spoon over the cauliflower. Scatter over the coriander leaves, cumin seeds and zhoug or chilli.

GREEK SALAD

Greek salad is a classic that can be served with any meal or as a meal on its own. Last time I went home it was served everywhere. This recipe is a modernised version of the classic.

500 g (1 lb 2 oz) mixed heirloom
   tomatoes, coarsely chopped
2 Lebanese (short) cucumbers,
   coarsely chopped
½ red onion, thinly sliced
50 g (1¾ oz) pitted black olives
40 g (1½ oz) pickled Middle Eastern
   or jalapeño chillies
3 tablespoons oregano leaves
juice of 1 lemon
100 ml (3½ fl oz) olive oil
300 g (10½ oz) feta cheese, cut into
   large cubes
black volcanic salt or sea salt flakes,
   to garnish

Put the tomatoes, cucumbers, onion, olives, chillies and oregano in a bowl and gently mix to combine. Pour in the lemon juice and half the oil and season with freshly ground black pepper.

Spoon the salad onto a platter and top with the feta. Drizzle with the remaining oil and garnish with the salt.

NOTE
I prefer soft Danish feta cheese but any other feta is also suitable.

Feasting

For us, eating is all about sharing – everyone filling
their plates with food from the centre of the table.
A feast is about conversation and community.
It is where people gather to celebrate milestones,
to share ideas – and food. There are recipes in this
chapter that can be prepared quickly, such as the
barbecued prawns with chermoula (see page 145),
which takes only a few minutes to cook. If you have
more time on your hands, you should try the baked
kefta (see page 121) or the 8-hour slow-roasted lamb
shoulder (see page 146) to take your shared table
to the next level.

SPICE-RUBBED ROAST LEG OF LAMB

Different rubs make the same main ingredient taste so different. For best results I recommend you marinate the leg of lamb in the fridge overnight but if you are pressed for time the minimum would be 4 hours. Bring it to room temperature before cooking.

2–2.5 kg (4 lb 8 oz–5 lb 8 oz) lamb leg

SPICY RUB
160 ml (5¼ fl oz) olive oil
5 cm (2 inch) piece ginger, grated
4 garlic cloves
3 teaspoons sea salt flakes
3 teaspoons sweet paprika
3 teaspoons fennel seeds, toasted
2 teaspoons ground cumin
2 teaspoons ground coriander
2 teaspoons chilli flakes
1½ teaspoons ground fenugreek
1 teaspoon ground black pepper
grated zest of 1 lemon

To make the spicy rub, put all the ingredients in a bowl and mix to combine.

Put the lamb on a rack in a large roasting tin. Using the tip of a sharp knife, make slits in the lamb to allow the rub to flavour the meat.

Massage the rub all over the lamb. Marinate in the fridge overnight or for at least 4 hours.

Preheat the oven to 190°C (375°F). Roast the lamb for 20 minutes, then reduce the temperature to 170°C (340°F) and roast for a further 35 minutes. Remove from the oven, cover with baking paper and foil and set aside to rest for at least 20 minutes.

To serve, carve the lamb into slices.

SAGE-ROASTED CHICKEN

Stuffed chicken was one of my favourite childhood dishes. This is a modernised, fancier version of the dish Mum used to cook. I find the sage gives the chicken a fragrant aroma that fills the whole house while it's roasting. If you don't like sage, you can use rosemary or any other type of sturdy herb.

1 large free-range chicken, around
    1.5 kg (3 lb 5 oz)
grated zest of 1 lemon
100 ml (3½ fl oz) olive oil
sea salt and cracked black pepper,
    for seasoning
5 bunches sage, for roasting

STUFFING

2 tablespoons olive oil
1 small brown onion, finely chopped
120 g (4¼ oz) minced (ground) veal
4 tablespoons pine nuts, lightly toasted
15 sage leaves, finely chopped

Preheat the oven to 190°C (375°F). Line a roasting tin with baking paper.

Wash the chicken and pat dry with paper towel. Set the chicken aside at room temperature while you prepare the stuffing.

To make the stuffing, heat the oil in a frying pan over medium heat. Cook the onion for 5 minutes, or until lightly golden. Add the veal and season with salt and freshly ground black pepper. Cook for 8–10 minutes, until the veal is cooked through. Remove from the heat and set aside to cool. Add the pine nuts and chopped sage leaves and mix together.

Stuff the chicken cavity with the veal mixture.

Combine the lemon zest with the olive oil, sea salt and cracked pepper, then rub the mixture over the whole chicken.

Spread the bunches of sage over the base of the roasting tin, then place the stuffed chicken on top. Bake for 45–50 minutes, until the chicken is cooked through.

KEFTA SENIEH (BAKED KEFTA)

Meatloaf fans will love this delicious layered variation on the traditional theme. I pre-cook the potatoes so the meat doesn't have to be overcooked, and you can serve the meat medium or well done, as you like it.

700 g (1 lb 9 oz) desiree (all-purpose) potatoes, peeled and cut into 1 cm (½ inch) slices

1 kg (2 lb 4 oz) coarsely minced (ground) lamb

1 teaspoon ground coriander

2 teaspoons ground cumin

1 teaspoon chilli flakes

4 tablespoons olive oil

2 large handfuls flat-leaf (Italian) parsley, leaves finely chopped, plus coarsely chopped leaves, extra, to garnish

1 small brown onion, finely chopped

2 teaspoons sea salt flakes

butter or olive oil, for greasing

4 tomatoes, thickly sliced

1 red onion, thickly sliced

400 g (10 oz) tin chopped tomatoes

2 tablespoons mild paprika

chopped coriander (cilantro) leaves, to garnish

Preheat the oven to 180°C (350°F).

Put the potato slices in a large saucepan and cover with cold water. Cook over medium heat until slightly softened, about 10 minutes. Drain and set aside.

Put the lamb mince, ground coriander, cumin, chilli flakes, olive oil, chopped parsley, onion and salt in a large bowl and mix by hand to combine. Roll the mince mixture into balls, about 60 g (2¼ oz) each, then flatten with your hands. (This shape helps the keftas sit upright when layered with the potato, tomato and onion.)

Grease a baking dish with butter (this will give a richer flavour to the dish) or olive oil. Layer the lamb kefta with the potato, tomato and red onion slices horizontally across the baking dish until all are used (see picture). Scatter any remaining onion rings over the top.

Put the tinned tomatoes and paprika in a small bowl. Mix and season with salt and freshly ground black pepper. Spoon this mixture over the layered kefta.

Cook in the oven for 40 minutes. Increase the temperature to 200°C (400°F) and cook for a further 15 minutes. (This will give the dish a nice colour.) Pour off a little of the cooking liquid.

Scatter with chopped parsley and coriander and serve in bowls.

BAKED WHOLE SNAPPER WITH WALNUTS, CHILLI AND TAHINI DRESSING

To work out how long to cook a whole fish in the oven, I allow three minutes per 100 g (3½ oz). So an 800 g (1 lb 12 oz) fish will require 24 minutes of baking time.

700–800 g (1 lb 9 oz–1 lb 12 oz) whole snapper, cleaned

4 tablespoons olive oil, plus 2 tablespoons extra

120 g (4¼ oz) walnuts, coarsely chopped

1 long green chilli, coarsely chopped (seeds optional)

1 teaspoon ground coriander

1 teaspoon ground cumin

2 large handfuls flat-leaf (Italian) parsley, leaves chopped

pinch of sea salt

4 tablespoons tahini dressing (see below)

Preheat the oven to 180°C (350°F).

Score the snapper on the diagonal 2–3 times on each side. Place on a baking tray lined with baking paper.

Put the 4 tablespoons of olive oil in a medium frying pan over medium heat. Add the walnuts and chilli and cook until lightly toasted. Add the coriander and cumin, stir and remove from the heat. Mix through the parsley, extra olive oil and salt.

Spread the walnut mixture over the snapper. Cook in the oven for 21–24 minutes, depending on the size of the fish. Serve on a platter with the tahini dressing on the side to spoon over.

TAHINI DRESSING
Put 2 peeled garlic cloves, 1 tablespoon sea salt flakes and 200 ml (7 fl oz) water in a food processor or blender, and blend to a paste. Add 280 g (10 oz) tahini and blend until combined. Transfer to a sterilised jar and store in the fridge for up to 7 days.

KIBBEH NEAH

'Neah' means 'raw' in Arabic, and this is the equivalent to the French steak tartare – which, as a chef, I like, because you can see the ingredients and the quality of the meat being served. I also think presenting this dish using a deconstructed approach is an elegant way to start a meal. In fact, it's a real showstopper. As you will be eating the meat raw, I recommend using only the best quality lamb for optimal flavour. I'd also just like to mention the burghul – it may seem like only a small quantity, but it will triple in size when blanched.

40 g (1½ oz) burghul (bulgur)

80 g (2¾ oz/⅔ cup) walnuts, finely crushed

2 tablespoons finely chopped flat-leaf (Italian) parsley

1 tablespoon finely chopped basil, plus extra leaves to garnish

1 teaspoon ground cumin

1 teaspoon ground cinnamon

1 teaspoon sea salt flakes

extra virgin olive oil, to drizzle

280 g (10 oz) good-quality lean lamb fillet or backstrap, cleaned

2 tablespoons pomegranate molasses

crisp pita bread (see Note) or lavosh, to serve

NOTE

To make crisp pita bread, tear the bread into rough pieces approximately 5 cm x 10 cm (2 inches x 4 inches). Deep fry 2 pieces of bread at a time in rice bran oil at 170°C (325°F) for 2–3 minutes. Drain and continue until all the bread is cooked. Sprinkle with 1 teaspoon sea salt flakes. Store in an airtight container lined with paper towel for up to 3 days.

Put the burghul in a bowl and rinse with plenty of hot water. Leave to soak for 2–3 minutes in hot water. Drain the burghul in a fine sieve or strainer, pressing down lightly to remove the water.

Spread the burghul out evenly on a baking tray and allow it to steam and cool to room temperature. Fluff up the burghul using your hands.

Put the burghul, walnuts, parsley, basil, cumin, cinnamon and half the salt in a large bowl. Add a drizzle of olive oil and combine gently with your hands. Set aside.

Mince the meat using the mincer attachment of an electric mixer set to the coarse setting. Alternatively, you can mince the meat by hand using a very sharp knife. Gently combine the minced lamb with the remaining salt and a drizzle of olive oil, taking care not to overmix. Set aside.

Spread out the seasoned burghul mixture on a serving plate. Create a sausage shape with the lamb mince and lay it over the burghul.

Drizzle the pomegranate molasses and some olive oil over the lamb and burghul.

At the table, gently mix the burghul and lamb mince together with two forks. Garnish with basil leaves and serve with crisp pita bread or lavosh.

Serves 4 as a main

CHICKEN CHERMOULA

I like to use metal skewers as they retain their heat and cook the centre of the chicken, but you can certainly use bamboo skewers. Soak them in water for a few minutes before using them; this will keep them from burning on the barbecue.

1 kg (2 lb 4 oz) boneless, skinless chicken thighs, cut into 3 cm x 3 cm (1¼ inch x 1¼ inch) pieces
2 tablespoons extra virgin olive oil
1 teaspoon sea salt flakes
1 tablespoon chopped coriander (cilantro) leaves

CHERMOULA

2 tablespoons cumin seeds
2 tablespoons coriander seeds
1 tablespoon caraway seeds
1 brown onion, coarsely chopped
4 garlic cloves, peeled
2 handfuls coriander (cilantro), leaves, stems and roots washed well
1 large green chilli
1 preserved lemon, skin only
3 teaspoons ground turmeric
2 tablespoons lemon juice
100 ml (3½ fl oz) olive oil

Prepare the chermoula. Heat a frying pan over medium heat and dry-fry the cumin, coriander and caraway seeds until fragrant, around 3 minutes. Using a food processor, grind the seeds coarsely.

Add the onion, garlic, coriander, chilli, preserved lemon and turmeric to the food processor and blend to a smooth paste. Add the lemon juice and blend for a further 2 minutes.

Scrape down the side of the bowl. Keep the motor running as you slowly drizzle in the olive oil. Season to taste.

Put the chicken pieces in a large bowl. Add 4 tablespoons chermoula, olive oil, salt and coriander and stir to combine. Cover and put in the fridge for 30 minutes to marinate.

Thread 3–4 pieces of chicken onto each skewer. Set aside until ready to cook.

Heat the barbecue to high and brush the grill with oil so the skewers won't stick. Cook the skewers for 3–4 minutes on each side.

NOTE

You can store the remaining chermoula in a sealed sterilised jar in the fridge for up to 2 weeks.

Clockwise from top centre:

Tabouleh (page 90),
za'atar bread (page 67),
chicken chermoula (page 125),
kibbeh neah (page 124),
crisp pita bread (page 124),
labneh (page 47).

SPINACH AND VEAL MEATBALLS

You can never have enough meatball recipes in your repertoire. This is a good midweek dinner as it is quick to prepare and is lovely with steamed rice. The veal mixture also makes great rissoles – roll it into patties and pan-fry them until cooked through.

2 large bunches English spinach
   (about 800 g/1 lb 12 oz), trimmed
500 g (1 lb 2 oz) minced (ground) veal
2 eggs
80 g (2¾ oz/⅔ cup) dry breadcrumbs
140 ml (4½ fl oz) olive oil
1 tablespoon dried mint (optional)
1 large brown onion, finely chopped
2 garlic cloves, crushed
4 tablespoons tomato paste
   (concentrated purée)
1 teaspoon chilli flakes
400 g (14 oz) tin chopped tomatoes
500 ml (17 fl oz/2 cups) beef stock
1 large handful coriander (cilantro),
   coarsely chopped

Bring a large saucepan of water to the boil. Fill a large bowl with ice and water. Add half the spinach to the boiling water and cook for 30 seconds, then transfer to the bowl of iced water. Repeat with the remaining spinach.

Drain the spinach and squeeze out all the liquid with your hands. Finely chop the spinach, then put it in a large bowl with the veal, eggs, breadcrumbs and 3 tablespoons of the olive oil. Add the mint, if using, and season with salt and freshly ground black pepper. Mix until well combined. Oil your hands and roll the veal mixture into balls about 55 g (2 oz) each, similar to the size of a golf ball.

Heat the remaining oil in a deep saucepan over medium heat. Cook the meatballs in batches for 2–3 minutes, until light golden brown (do not cook through as they will finish cooking in the sauce).

Remove from the pan and set aside.

Add the onion and garlic to the pan and sweat for 3–5 minutes. Add the tomato paste and chilli flakes and cook for another minute. Stir in the chopped tomatoes and stock and bring to the boil. Reduce the heat to medium–low and carefully add the meatballs. Simmer for 25–30 minutes, until the meatballs are cooked through. Season with salt and pepper. Just before serving, stir in the chopped coriander.

BAKED RAINBOW TROUT WITH TAHINI AND PINE NUTS

Growing up beside the beach, we used to be able to get a lot of fresh fish from the local port. Cooking fish was the one thing my mum wasn't very good at doing in the kitchen, but somehow she was capable of perfecting this dish. This recipe uses rainbow trout, which is a beautiful fish available widely where we live, but feel free to use whatever fish is local to you.

2 rainbow trout, about 450–500 g
    (1 lb–1 lb 2 oz) each, scaled
    and gutted
4 tablespoons olive oil
270 g (9½ oz/1 cup) tahini
2 garlic cloves, crushed
4 tablespoons pine nuts, toasted
3 tablespoons chopped flat-leaf
    (Italian) parsley
1 large fresh red chilli, finely chopped

Preheat the oven to 190°C (375°F). Line a baking tray with baking paper.

Put the rainbow trout on the tray. Drizzle with 3 tablespoons of the oil and season with salt and freshly ground black pepper. Bake for 15–20 minutes, until done to your liking.

Put the tahini in a bowl with the garlic and 250 ml (9 fl oz/1 cup) water. Season with salt and whisk until smooth. Pour this mixture over the cooked fish and bake for 1 minute, just until the tahini is lukewarm (overheating the tahini will cause it to curdle).

Serve the fish garnished with the pine nuts, parsley and chilli and drizzled with the remaining olive oil.

DUKKAH LAMB CUTLETS WITH MINT AND POMEGRANATE SALAD

It is so easy to put this dish together, and yet it makes such a big impact with its sharp, clean flavours.

3 tablespoons olive oil

6 tablespoons hazelnut dukkah (see page 46)

8 large lamb cutlets (or lamb chops or noisettes)

MINT AND POMEGRANATE SALAD

1 handful mint leaves

4 tablespoons pomegranate seeds

1 preserved lemon, skin only, julienned

juice of ½ a lemon

3 tablespoons olive oil

Put the olive oil and dukkah in a large bowl and mix together. Add the lamb and rub the dukkah mixture into the meat. Cover the bowl and transfer to the fridge to marinate for 30 minutes.

To make the salad, put the mint, pomegranate seeds and preserved lemon in a bowl. Shake together the lemon juice and olive oil in a small jar. Pour over the salad, toss gently and season with salt and freshly ground black pepper, taking care not to use too much salt as there is salt in the dukkah on the cutlets.

Heat the barbecue to high or heat a chargrill pan over high heat on your stovetop. Cook the lamb cutlets for 2–3 minutes on each side. Remove the pan from the heat and rest the lamb for 5 minutes before serving with the mint and pomegranate salad.

Serves 4–6

CHICKEN, NOODLE AND LEEK SOUP

There is nothing that chicken soup can't heal, it is said, and it's one of those dishes you can eat at any time of the day.

3 tablespoons olive oil

2 garlic cloves, crushed

1 leek, white part and half of the green part, rinsed and thinly sliced

100 g (3½ oz) kugel, egg or vermicelli noodles

sea salt and white pepper, to season

1 small handful flat-leaf (Italian) parsley, finely chopped

STOCK

1 small (about 1.2 kg/2 lb 10 oz) chicken

1 brown onion, finely chopped

3 garlic cloves, crushed, plus 5 peeled cloves, extra

2 celery stalks

1 carrot

2 fresh or dried bay leaves

½ teaspoon white peppercorns

To make the stock, put all of the ingredients in a large saucepan with 5 litres (175 fl oz/20 cups) water. Simmer over medium heat for 45 minutes.

Remove the saucepan from the heat and transfer the chicken to a chopping board. When cool enough to handle, pull the chicken meat off the carcass and shred with your hands. Cover and set aside until you are ready to serve the soup. Discard the chicken carcass. Strain the stock and set aside. Discard the vegetables.

To make the soup, put the olive oil and garlic in a large saucepan over medium heat and cook for 1–2 minutes. Add the leek and cook for 3–4 minutes. Add 1 litre (35 fl oz/4 cups) of the reserved chicken stock. Turn the heat up to high and bring to the boil. Add the noodles and cook according to the packet instructions, or approximately 5 minutes, stirring from time to time.

Add the shredded chicken to the noodles and stock and cook for 4–5 minutes, just to warm through and meld the flavours. Season with sea salt and white pepper. Stir through the parsley and serve.

LAMB KEFTA

Kids love these meatballs, and they make a good meat dish if you are trying to introduce new flavours. When my niece and nephews come over for dinner, they work out how many keftas each person should get and always make sure they eat their share! Luckily this recipe can easily be doubled, tripled ... Serve your kefta with hummus, tabouleh and pita bread for a light meal, or make it part of your shared table.

500 g (1 lb 2 oz) good-quality minced (ground) lamb
75 g (2½ oz) pine nuts
1 teaspoon ground cumin
¼ teaspoon ground cinnamon
1 handful flat-leaf (Italian) parsley or coriander (cilantro), leaves coarsely chopped
2 tablespoons good-quality olive oil
3 tablespoons olive oil, for frying
pine nuts, to garnish (optional)

Put the minced lamb, pine nuts, cumin, cinnamon, parsley or coriander and good-quality olive oil in a large bowl. Combine well with your hands. Form small round balls of mince mixture then flatten to make small hamburger shapes. Set aside in the fridge until ready to cook.

Heat the olive oil for frying in a large frying pan over medium heat. Cook the kefta in batches for 3 minutes on each side, moving them around in the pan, taking care not to overcook them. Keep the kefta warm on a plate covered with foil until all are cooked.

Garnish with pine nuts (optional) and serve with hummus (see page 44), tabouleh and pita bread (see page 65).

LENTIL RICE (MUJADDARA)

Serves 6–8 as a side dish

Mujaddara – which translates as 'jewelled rice' – works really well on its own or with a protein dish. When Mum had cooked the mujaddara and was preparing the rest of dinner, we kids would sneak into the kitchen, take a big spoonful and add a dollop of yoghurt for a snack. It's also a great vegetarian dish with salads.

215 g (7½ oz/1 cup) green lentils
3 tablespoons olive oil, plus 125 ml
  (4 fl oz/½ cup) olive oil, extra
400 g (14 oz/2 cups) basmati or
  jasmine rice
1 tablespoon ground cumin
1 teaspoon sea salt
750 ml (26 fl oz/3 cups) boiling water
2 brown onions, thinly sliced
1 handful flat-leaf (Italian) parsley,
  leaves chopped
100 g (3½ oz/⅔ cup) pine nuts, toasted

Put the lentils and 1.25 litres (44 fl oz/5 cups) cold water in a large saucepan over medium heat. Bring to the boil then reduce the heat to a gentle simmer and cook for 18 minutes, or until the lentils are soft but not mushy. Drain and set aside.

Heat the 3 tablespoons of olive oil in a medium saucepan over medium heat. Add the rice and toss lightly until it warms through. Add the cumin and salt and mix through. Add the boiling water and bring to the boil. Cover the saucepan with a lid, reduce the heat to low and cook for 18 minutes. Remove the saucepan from the heat and let the rice rest for 5 minutes with the lid on. Remove the lid and fluff the rice with a fork.

Put the 125 ml of oil in a frying pan over medium–high heat. Cook the onion until golden brown and slightly crispy, taking care not to overcook it.

Put the lentils, rice, onion, parsley and pine nuts in a large bowl and gently fold with a fork to combine.

Clockwise from top left:

Claudia's chopped vegetable salad (page 102),
lamb kefta (page 136),
lentil rice (page 137),
hummus (page 44)

CHICKEN MEATBALLS WITH SILVERBEET AND TOMATO

I have earned lots of brownie points from my nieces and nephews for serving up these meatballs. Eaten with rice or tossed through pasta, they are packed with vegetables and protein – and they're delicious.

1 kg (2 lb 4 oz) minced (ground) chicken

1 large handful coriander (cilantro), leaves chopped

100 g (3½ oz) fresh or dry breadcrumbs

3 eggs

3 tablespoons extra virgin olive oil

½ teaspoon freshly ground black pepper

1½ tablespoons sea salt

4 tablespoons olive oil

1 large brown onion, finely chopped

5 garlic cloves, diced

2 large red chillies, chopped (optional)

2 x 400 g (14 oz) tins crushed tomatoes

500 ml (17 fl oz/2 cups) chicken stock

200 g (7 oz) silverbeet (Swiss chard) leaves, coarsely chopped

rice or pasta, to serve

Put the chicken mince in a large bowl with the coriander, breadcrumbs, eggs, extra virgin olive oil, pepper and salt. Mix to combine, then form the mixture into golf-ball-sized balls.

Heat the olive oil in a large saucepan over medium–high heat. Cook the chicken balls until just golden brown in three batches. (They will cook all the way through in the tomato sauce in the next step.) Transfer the chicken balls to a bowl and set aside.

Add the onion, garlic and chilli, if using, to the saucepan and cook over medium heat for 5 minutes, until softened. Add the tomatoes and stock and bring to the boil. Return the browned chicken balls to the saucepan and cook for 35–40 minutes over medium heat.

Add the silverbeet in three batches, allowing the leaves to steam with the lid on and cook down after each addition. Season with salt and freshly ground black pepper to taste and cook for a further 5 minutes, or until the silverbeet has wilted into the sauce.

Serve with rice or pasta of your choice.

LAMB AND CHICKPEA STEW

Warm and comforting, this is just like the stew my mum made when I was growing up. Serve it with couscous like she did for an even more hearty meal.

⅔ cup (170 ml) olive oil

1 kg (2 lb 4 oz) lamb shanks

2 litres (70 fl oz/8 cups) good-quality vegetable stock

2 small brown onions, coarsely chopped

3 garlic cloves

3 celery stalks, coarsely chopped

2 red chillies, finely chopped

1 tablespoon ground turmeric

2 tablespoons coriander seeds

2 tablespoons cumin seeds

400 g (14 oz) tin chickpeas, drained

1 litre (35 fl oz/4 cups) stock reserved from cooking the lamb shanks

1 handful coriander (cilantro), leaves picked

Heat 4 tablespoons of the olive oil in a large saucepan over medium heat. Sear the lamb shanks on each side until well coloured. Add the vegetable stock and bring to the boil. Reduce to a simmer, cover with a lid and cook for 3 hours, or until the shank meat falls off the bone, skimming the surface from time to time. Set aside to cool a little.

When the lamb shanks are cool enough to handle, take the meat off them and break it into big chunks. Reserve the stock.

Put the remaining olive oil in a large saucepan over medium heat. Cook the onion and garlic for 5 minutes, or until softened. Add the celery and chilli and cook for 3–4 minutes. Add the turmeric and coriander and cumin seeds and cook for 2 minutes. Add the chickpeas and the reserved lamb shank stock and cook for 25 minutes. Season with sea salt to taste.

Add the shredded lamb to the chickpea stew and cook over low heat for 10 minutes.

To serve, ladle the stew into large bowls and garnish with the coriander leaves.

Serves 4–6

BARBECUED PRAWNS WITH CHERMOULA

As a chef, I've noticed that friends are reluctant to invite me over for a meal. Perhaps they think they need to cook something fancy or complicated to impress me, but that's not the case. One night, Kristy and I were invited to a friend's house for dinner where we were served fresh cooked prawns, soft white rolls and a good-quality mayonnaise. We were in food heaven! The simple things in life tend to be the best, and this is definitely true of food. These prawns prove you don't need to slave over a stove to impress. They're great as a fancy finger food or can be served with other dishes as a main meal.

1 kg (2 lb 4 oz) large raw prawns
   (shrimp), about 20–25 prawns
5 tablespoons chermoula (page 125)
3 tablespoons olive oil, plus extra
   for drizzling
20 basil leaves, coarsely chopped

Heat the barbecue or a chargrill pan to high.

Put the prawns in a large bowl. Add the chermoula and olive oil and mix to combine.

Cook the prawns in batches on the hot barbecue or chargrill pan for 1 minute on each side, or until done to your liking.

Arrange the cooked prawns on a platter. Drizzle with olive oil, season with salt and freshly ground black pepper and scatter with the basil.

8-HOUR SLOW-ROASTED LAMB SHOULDER

Slow-roasting meat is meant to be easy, and this recipe proves that it can be. All you need to do is combine the ingredients, cover the lamb, put it in the oven and let the magic happen.

2 tablespoons coriander seeds, lightly toasted
100 ml (3½ fl oz) olive oil
1 tablespoon sea salt flakes
½ tablespoon freshly ground black pepper
1 lamb shoulder, bone in, about 2 kg (4 lb 8 oz)
1 garlic bulb, cut in half horizontally

Preheat the oven to 180°C (350°F).

Use a mortar and pestle to lightly bruise the toasted coriander seeds. Transfer to a small bowl and add the olive oil, salt and pepper. Stir to combine.

Rub the mixture over the lamb shoulder.

Put the lamb in a roasting tin with the garlic. Cover the lamb with baking paper. Wrap a layer of foil tightly over the lamb and the edge of the roasting tin so that no steam can escape during cooking and the lamb cooks in its own juices. Cook for 2 hours. Reduce the temperature to 120°C (235°F) and cook for a further 6 hours.

The meat is cooked when it pulls away from the bone easily. At this point, increase the oven temperature to 200°C (400°F). Remove the foil and baking paper and cook the meat for a further 10 minutes to crisp up and colour the outside of the lamb.

Serve the lamb with any or all of the dishes in the banquet on pages 148–149.

Serves 6–8

CHICKEN BASTILLA

A Moroccan festive dish, bastilla combines the sweet and the salty. It's not unusual to see cinnamon used with meat and other savoury dishes in Mediterranean cooking, and it works really well in this savoury pie, where it's used to add sweetness along with the icing sugar that is sprinkled on top. For a special occasion, cut out a stencil and dust with the icing sugar to create a pattern.

65 g (2¼ oz/½ cup) slivered almonds
70 g (2½ oz/½ cup) pistachio nut
    kernels
3 tablespoons olive oil
1 brown onion, finely chopped
2 garlic cloves, finely chopped
1 teaspoon ground cinnamon,
    plus extra, for sprinkling
1 teaspoon finely grated ginger
2 teaspoons ground cumin
2 teaspoons ground coriander
2 teaspoons fennel seeds
4 boneless, skinless chicken breasts
    (about 600 g/1 lb 5 oz), minced
    (ground)
pinch of saffron threads, soaked in
    2 tablespoons hot water
1 egg, lightly beaten
1 handful coriander (cilantro) leaves,
    coarsely chopped
120 g (4¼ oz) butter, melted
15 sheets (about 300 g/10½ oz)
    filo pastry
icing (confectioners') sugar,
    for sprinkling

Preheat the oven to 220°C (425°F). Put the almonds and pistachios on a baking tray and toast in the oven for 5 minutes, or until the almonds get a bit of colour. Transfer the nuts to a food processor (leave the oven on) and pulse until coarsely ground. Set aside.

Heat the olive oil in a large frying pan over medium–high heat. Add the onion and garlic and cook for 3–4 minutes. Add the cinnamon, ginger, cumin, coriander and fennel seeds and cook for 1 minute. Add the chicken and cook for 5 minutes. Remove the pan from the heat and stir through the saffron and its soaking water. Set aside to cool.

Season the cooled chicken mixture with salt and freshly ground black pepper. Add the beaten egg and chopped coriander. Mix to combine.

Grease a round 24 cm (9½ inch) cake tin with butter. Lay a sheet of filo pastry in the tin; it will hang over the edge. Brush with melted butter and scatter over a thin layer of the nut mixture. Add the next layer of filo in the opposite direction (you are going to fold all of these layers over to seal the pie). Repeat with the filo, butter and nuts until you have used all but 1 sheet of the filo.

Spoon the chicken mixture on top of the layered filo. Press down the chicken evenly. Bring each filo layer onto the top of the pie, closing it up, adding melted butter and nuts to each layer as you do.

Bake the bastilla for 20 minutes. Reduce the oven temperature to 180°C (350°F). Take the pie out of the oven and flip it out onto a baking tray. Cook for a further 10 minutes or until it has a good colour on all sides. Serve sprinkled with icing sugar and cinnamon.

Clockwise from left:

Beetroot pickled cucumbers (page 78),
green olives, white anchovies and
coriander seeds (page 49),
8-hour slow-roasted lamb shoulder (page 146),
cauliflower and cranberry salad (page 101),
warm Moroccan carrot salad (page 98),
chicken bastilla (page 147)

STUFFED SPATCHCOCKS WITH LAMB AND PINE NUTS

One of my mum's favourites for when guests come over, this dish is big on the wow factor and absolutely delicious, too.

3 tablespoons olive oil

2 brown onions, finely diced

3 garlic cloves, crushed

¼ teaspoon ground cinnamon

¼ teaspoon freshly grated nutmeg

¼ teaspoon allspice

500 g (1 lb 2 oz) minced (ground) lamb

50 g (1¾ oz/⅓ cup) pine nuts, toasted

4 x 500 g (1 lb 2 oz) spatchcocks

MARINADE

125 ml (4 fl oz/½ cup) olive oil

2 teaspoons allspice

1 tablespoon pomegranate molasses

Preheat the oven to 180°C (350°F). Line a baking tray with baking paper.

Heat the olive oil in a medium frying pan over medium heat. Add the onion and garlic and cook for 3–4 minutes. Add the cinnamon, nutmeg and allspice and cook for a further 1–2 minutes. Add the lamb mince and stir occasionally until cooked. Season with salt and freshly ground black pepper to taste. Remove from the heat, add the pine nuts and mix to combine.

Rinse the cavity of each spatchcock with cold water and pat dry with paper towel. Stuff the cavities with the mince mixture. You can push a toothpick through the cavity wall to secure it (but don't forget to remove it before serving).

To make the marinade, mix the olive oil, allspice and pomegranate molasses together. Rub it over the spatchcocks.

Put the spatchcocks on the prepared tray and cook for 40–45 minutes. Remove from the oven and leave to rest for 5–10 minutes.

Serve on a large platter.

Serves 6

TOMATO FISH STEW

Chreime is a North African-Jewish fish stew that's delicious with sweet bread such as challah or brioche to dip into the spicy, tomatoey sauce. I like to use barramundi for this, as the earthiness works well with the spices, but you can use any white-fleshed fish.

3 tablespoons olive oil

2 large red capsicums (peppers), seeds removed and cut into strips

8 garlic cloves, coarsely chopped

1 green chilli, chopped (seeds optional)

3 ripe tomatoes, diced

2 tablespoons smoked paprika

2 teaspoons ground cumin

400 ml (14 fl oz) fish stock

6 white-fleshed fish fillets (about 1.2 kg/2 lb 8 oz)

1 large handful coriander (cilantro), leaves coarsely chopped

Heat the olive oil in a deep frying pan with a lid over medium heat. Cook the capsicum and garlic for 5 minutes, or until fragrant and slightly softened. Add the chilli and cook for 1 minute. Add the tomato and cook for 5 minutes. Add the paprika and cumin, stir and cook for another 2 minutes. Add the fish stock, reduce the heat to medium–low and cook for 15 minutes. Check the seasoning and adjust with salt if necessary.

Add the fish to the stew, skin side up. Cover the frying pan and cook over medium–low heat for 10 minutes. Remove the lid and let the sauce simmer for 5 minutes. If necessary, you can increase or decrease this cooking time by 2–4 minutes according to the size of the fish fillets. Add the coriander and serve at the table from the frying pan.

Serves 4

LAMB BURGERS WITH MIDDLE EASTERN COLESLAW

Including your guests in the preparation of a meal is a great way to entertain, and these burgers are ideal for a lunch party where you get the ingredients ready beforehand, and lay them on the table for all to make their own.

750 g (1 lb 10 oz) good-quality coarsely minced (ground) lamb

2 teaspoons coriander seeds, toasted and crushed

1 handful coriander (cilantro), leaves finely chopped

3 tablespoons olive oil

5 tablespoons red harissa (see page 68)

1 teaspoon chilli flakes

4 tablespoons aïoli, to serve

4 brioche burger buns, toasted

MIDDLE EASTERN COLESLAW

½ red cabbage

2 carrots

sea salt flakes

1 handful mint, leaves picked

2 large handfuls flat-leaf (Italian) parsley, leaves finely chopped

1 handful coriander (cilantro), leaves coarsely chopped

100 ml (3½ fl oz) extra virgin olive oil

4 tablespoons husroum (verjuice)

Prepare the coleslaw. Use a mandolin or knife to shave the cabbage finely and julienne the carrots. Place in a large bowl, sprinkle with sea salt flakes and press down on the cabbage and carrot with your hands to soften them.

Add the mint, parsley and coriander to the bowl and mix well. Add the olive oil and husroum, and season with freshly ground black pepper. Toss to combine and set aside.

Put the minced lamb, coriander seeds, chopped coriander, olive oil, 4 tablespoons of the harissa and the chilli flakes in a large bowl.

Season with salt and freshly ground black pepper and mix to combine.

Divide the meat mixture into four equal portions and gently shape into burger patties with your hands. (Don't overwork the patties as the meat will become tough.)

Cook the burgers in a non-stick frying pan over medium heat for 2–3 minutes each side (for medium–rare), or to your taste. You can also cook them using the grill (broiler) or barbecue heated to medium.

Combine the aïoli and remaining harissa in a small bowl.

To assemble the burgers, toast the cut side of the buns. Place the bun bottoms on plates and add a dollop of the harissa aïoli, a handful of coleslaw and a pattie. Add another handful of coleslaw and dollop of aïoli and top with the bun lid.

Dessert

Middle Eastern desserts tend to be very sweet and syrupy, and they're enjoyed at various points of the day rather than after a big meal. If you have guests over, you might serve dried fruits, nuts and mint tea after dinner but not cake, which is a Western custom. In this chapter, we've married the Western idea of dessert after dinner with the Middle Eastern flavour palate. There are treats to serve during the day, such as the almond and coconut cake (see page 176), and delicious desserts like the layered Turkish delight pavlova (see page 180). We've also included our signature Kepos Street churros (see page 183) – always a favourite.

Serves 8–10

APPLE, DATE AND HONEY CAKE

My apple, date and honey cake requires minimal effort but has maximum impact. The apples can be replaced with pears, apricots, figs or poached quinces, and the dates can be swapped for any other dried fruit.

oil spray for greasing
200 g (7 oz) butter
120 g (4¼ oz) almond meal
80 g (2¾ oz) plain (all-purpose) flour, sifted
10 dried dates, pitted and coarsely chopped
6 egg whites
220 g (7 oz/1 cup) caster (superfine) sugar
30 g (1 oz) flaked almonds
4 tablespoons honey (optional, see Notes)

CARAMEL APPLES

60 g (2¼ oz) caster (superfine) sugar
2 tablespoons honey
30 g (1 oz) butter, cubed
3 large red apples, peeled, cored and cut into 8 wedges

NOTES

You can use the leftover liquid from the caramel apples to drizzle over the cooked cake instead of using honey.

You can also make this into a slice by cooking it in a 20 x 30 cm (8 x 12 inch) cake tin.

Preheat the oven to 170°C (340°F). Spray a 24 cm (9½ inch) springform cake tin with oil and line the base with baking paper. Spray the paper with oil.

To make the caramel apples, put the sugar and honey in a large frying pan. Cook over medium heat, stirring occasionally, until the mixture forms a golden caramel – about 8–10 minutes. Add the butter and stir until melted. Add the apple wedges and cook for 5–8 minutes, until the apples are golden and the sugar syrup is sticky. Stir only once or twice during cooking so they don't break up. Remove from the heat and set aside to cool to room temperature.

To make the cake batter, cook the butter in a separate frying pan over medium heat for 10–12 minutes, until golden brown. Remove from the heat and set aside.

Put the almond meal, flour and dates in a bowl. Stir until the dates have separated and are evenly coated in the almond meal and flour.

Using an electric mixer fitted with a whisk attachment, whisk the egg whites until soft peaks form. Gradually add the sugar and whisk until medium peaks form, about 5 minutes.

Gently pour the browned butter over the date mixture and stir to combine, then fold in the egg white mixture.

Pour the batter into the prepared tin. Arrange the cooked apple wedges on top, trying not to add any excess liquid (reserve the liquid to drizzle over the cooked cake). Scatter the flaked almonds over the apple and bake for 30–35 minutes, until the cake is golden and cooked through. Remove from the oven and cool in the tin for 20 minutes.

Drizzle the honey or reserved caramel over the cake and serve warm or at room temperature.

BANANA KATAIFI TARTE TATIN

Tarte tatin is one of my favourite desserts. This one is a playful twist on the classic and the kataifi pastry gives it a crisper base. It's a fantastic dessert for entertaining as you can have most of the preparation done in advance and bake it when you're ready for dessert. It's delicious with vanilla or chocolate ice cream. You can change the fruit to apples, pears, peaches or apricots, or any other fruit that will hold its shape when cooked. You could also scatter crumbled pistachio nuts over the bananas for a Greek kataifi dessert effect.

220 g (7¾ oz/1 cup) caster (superfine) sugar
50 g (1¾ oz) butter
150 g (5½ oz) kataifi pastry
60 g (2¼ oz) butter, melted
6–8 bananas, cut into 3 cm (1¼ inch) pieces

Preheat the oven to 170°C (340°F).

Heat a 24 cm (9½ inch) ovenproof frying pan over medium–low heat. Add the sugar and 50 ml (1½ fl oz) of water and cook, swirling the pan without stirring, for 7–8 minutes, until the caramel turns a nut-brown colour. Add the butter and stir to combine. Remove the pan from the heat and set aside.

Put the kataifi pastry in a large bowl and gently separate the strands with your hands. Pour in the melted butter and gently mix through.

Carefully arrange the banana pieces in the pan with the caramel. Spread the kataifi pastry over the top of the banana in an even layer. Press down and flatten the pastry, then bake for 20–25 minutes, until golden brown.

To serve, carefully turn the tarte tatin out onto a large plate.

DATE AND DUKKAH BROWNIES

It may seem an unusual pairing, but dates and dukkah work well together in these brownies to create a salty and sweet taste sensation.

350 g (12 oz) pitted dates, coarsely chopped (or leave whole)

3 tablespoons hazelnut dukkah (see page 46)

300 g (10½ oz) bitter dark chocolate, coarsely chopped

80 g (2¾ oz) unsalted butter

4 eggs, whisked

300 g (10½ oz) caster (superfine) sugar

55 g (2 oz) plain (all-purpose) flour

3 tablespoons unsweetened cocoa powder, plus extra for dusting

2 teaspoons baking powder

100 g (3½ oz) sour cream

150 g (5½ oz/1 cup) dark chocolate melts

Preheat the oven to 170°C (325°F). Line a 20 cm x 30 cm (8 inch x 12 inch) baking tin with baking paper.

Put the dates, dukkah and 200 ml (7 fl oz) water in a medium saucepan over medium–high heat and bring to the boil. Set aside to cool. (This step can be done in advance.)

Put the chopped chocolate and butter in a heatproof bowl over a saucepan of simmering water, making sure that the water doesn't touch the base of the bowl. Stir until melted. Alternatively, melt the chocolate and butter in a microwave. Set aside to cool to room temperature.

Put the egg and sugar in a large bowl and mix until smooth. Add the cooled chocolate and butter mixture and stir until combined.

Sift together the flour, cocoa powder and baking powder into a medium bowl. Add to the chocolate mixture and stir with a wooden spoon. Add the sour cream, chocolate melts and date and dukkah mixture, including the cooking liquid, and mix to combine.

Pour the mixture into the prepared tin. Bake for 40 minutes, or until set.

Allow the brownie to cool for at least 3 hours or until it is firm enough to cut. Dust with cocoa powder and cut into 16 squares.

MICHAL'S BABKA

This recipe was given to me by my friend Michal, who helped when we were setting up Kepos Street Kitchen. She made these babkas when we first opened, and the smell of them baking reminded me of the streets of Tel Aviv on a Friday afternoon, when most pastry shops would be cooking these cakes to get ready for the weekend.

500 g (1 lb 2 oz/3⅓ cups) self-raising flour, plus extra for dusting
25 g (1 oz) dried yeast
100 g (3½ oz) unsalted butter, melted
115 g (4 oz) caster (superfine) sugar
3 tablespoons canola oil
2 eggs
90 ml (3 fl oz) lukewarm water

FILLING
190 g (6¾ oz) caster (superfine) sugar
25 g (1 oz) unsweetened cocoa powder
65 g (2¼ oz) unsalted butter, at room temperature
3 tablespoons boiling water

To make the dough, put the flour, yeast, butter, sugar, oil, eggs and lukewarm water in a large bowl and mix to combine. Knead the mixture vigorously by hand on a lightly floured work surface for at least 10 minutes. Alternatively, use an electric mixer with a dough hook and mix for at least 6 minutes, or until the dough is smooth and sticky. (Stay close to the electric mixer to keep it steady as it will jump around while mixing this dough.)

Transfer the dough to a large clean bowl, dust the top with flour and cover the bowl with a damp tea towel (dish towel). Leave to prove in a warm place for at least 40 minutes, or until doubled in size.

Meanwhile, make the filling. Put the sugar, cocoa, butter and boiling water in a medium bowl and mix to combine.

Line a baking tray with baking paper. Dust a work surface with flour and roll out the proven dough to a large rectangle, approximately 5 mm (¼ inch) thick. Spread the filling over the dough, leaving a 1 cm (½ inch) border around the edge. Starting from the long edge closest to you, tightly roll the dough into a cylinder. Cut the cylinder into 12 equal portions. Place the babkas evenly on the prepared tray, 3 across and 4 down, leaving enough space in between for the babkas to double in size. Cover with a damp tea towel and leave to rise again for 40 minutes, or until doubled in size.

Preheat the oven to 180°C (350°F).

Bake for 30–40 minutes, or until golden. Serve warm.

Clockwise from top left:

Kristy's famous caramel slice (page 166),
Michal's babka (page 163),
mini fig and walnut cakes with
mascarpone cheese (page 167),
date and dukkah brownies (page 162),
Persian meringue cake (page 168),
almond and coconut cake (page 176).

KRISTY'S FAMOUS CARAMEL SLICE

Even though it isn't a Middle Eastern slice, this classic has become a regular part of the cake display at Kepos Street Kitchen. Kristy's version uses maple syrup, which adds an elegant depth of flavour.

BASE

300 g (10½ oz/2 cups) plain
   (all-purpose) flour
90 g (3¼ oz/1 cup) desiccated coconut
185 g (6½ oz/1 cup, lightly packed)
   dark brown sugar
250 g (9 oz) butter, melted

CARAMEL

175 g (6 oz/½ cup) maple syrup or
   golden syrup
175 g (6 oz) butter, melted
3 x 395 g (14 oz) tins sweetened
   condensed milk

CHOCOLATE TOPPING

250 g (9 oz) good-quality dark
   chocolate, coarsely chopped
4 tablespoons light olive oil

Preheat the oven to 180°C (350°F). Line a 20 cm x 30 cm (8 inch x 12 inch) cake tin with baking paper, allowing it to overhang at the ends for easy removal of the slice.

To make the base, put the flour, coconut, sugar and melted butter in a medium bowl and combine. Spread over the base of the tin and press in evenly using the back of a spoon. Bake for 15 minutes.

Meanwhile, prepare the caramel. Put the maple syrup, melted butter and sweetened condensed milk in a large heavy-based saucepan over medium–low heat and cook, stirring constantly, for 5–7 minutes, or until it starts to thicken.

When the base is cooked, pour the caramel over it and bake for 20 minutes, or until the caramel is a light golden brown. Cool the slice to room temperature and put in the fridge overnight.

When the chilled caramel is firm, make the chocolate topping. Put the chocolate in a bowl and melt in the microwave. Add the olive oil and stir until very smooth. Pour the melted chocolate over the caramel and return to the fridge for 5–10 hours, until firm.

When set, lift the slice out of the tin and cut into 20 pieces.

Makes 8–10

MINI FIG AND WALNUT CAKES WITH MASCARPONE CHEESE

The fig and walnut flavours go so well together in these lovely little cakes. You can make this recipe using a regular muffin or mini kugelhopf tray instead of the mini bundt tray we used here.

150 g (5½ oz) walnuts
110 g (3¾ oz/¾ cup) self-raising flour
75 g (2½ oz/½ cup) plain
   (all-purpose) flour
250 g (9 oz) unsalted butter,
   cut into cubes, at room temperature
100 g (3½ oz) caster (superfine) sugar
80 g (2¾ oz) fig jam
3 eggs

TOPPING
250 g (9 oz) mascarpone cheese
250 ml (9 fl oz/1 cup) thin (pouring)
   cream
50 g (1¾ oz) icing (confectioners') sugar
5 fresh figs
50 g (1¾ oz) honey

Preheat the oven to 180°C (350°F). Thoroughly grease 10 holes of a mini bundt tray to prevent the cakes sticking when turned out.

Put the walnuts and self-raising and plain flours in a food processor and blend to a fine powder.

Using an electric mixer with the whisk attachment, cream the butter and sugar until pale and creamy. Add the jam and whisk for 2 minutes. Add the eggs one at a time, whisking well after each addition, and then whisk for an extra 2 minutes, or until really well combined. Fold in the walnut powder and mix until just combined.

Spoon the mixture into the tray, filling the holes to two-thirds of the way up. Bake for 20–25 minutes. Cool for 2–3 minutes in the tray then turn out onto a wire rack to cool.

To make the topping, put the mascarpone cheese, cream and icing sugar in a medium bowl and whisk until very thick, without overmixing.

Break the figs in half by hand. Spoon a dollop of cream onto each cake, and top with a fig half and a drizzle of honey.

PERSIAN MERINGUE CAKE

An unconventional pavlova that's perfect as a celebration cake, this was created accidentally one day at Kepos Street Kitchen when we were trying to make a unique gluten-free cake for a customer. It is a versatile recipe so you can change the type of nuts and berries you use – don't be afraid to put your own stamp on it. You can also make it look more like a regular pavlova by omitting the glaze and adding cream, fresh nuts and pomegranate seeds. It can be made up to 5 days in advance – just glaze it on the day you want to eat it.

6 egg whites, at room temperature
200 g (7 oz) caster (superfine) sugar
500 g (1 lb 2 oz) plain halva, diced into
 1 cm (½ inch) cubes
200 g (7 oz) pitted dates, chopped
200 g (7 oz) dried barberries or
 cranberries
125 g (4½ oz/1¼ cups) almond meal
50 g (1¾ oz) pistachio nut kernels,
 coarsely chopped
50 g (1¾ oz) blanched whole almonds,
 coarsely chopped
120 g (4¼ oz) white chocolate chips
1 teaspoon rosewater
shaved halva, chopped pistachio nut
 kernels, pomegranate seeds or rose
 petals dusted with sugar, to garnish
 (optional)

WHITE CHOCOLATE GLAZE

75 ml (2¼ fl oz) thin (pouring) cream
150 g (5½ oz) white chocolate, coarsely
 chopped

Preheat the oven to 160°C (315°F). Grease a 24 cm (9½ inch) springform cake tin with butter and line the base with baking paper.

Using an electric mixer with the whisk attachment, whisk the egg whites on high speed until soft peaks form. Gradually add the sugar, whisking until the mixture is firm and glossy as you would with a meringue.

Gently fold in the halva, dates, berries, almond meal, pistachios, almonds, chocolate chips and rosewater. Spoon the mixture into the prepared tin. Bake for 1 hour, or until the cake is firm to the touch. Set aside to cool completely in the tin on a wire rack.

To make the glaze, put the cream and chocolate in a small saucepan over low heat and stir until melted. Remove from the heat and set aside to cool, stirring every 2 minutes to prevent lumps forming.

When ready to serve, remove the springform ring and spoon the glaze over the pavlova. Scatter over a Middle Eastern garnish, such as shaved halva, chopped pistachio nut kernels, pomegranate seeds or rose petals dusted with sugar, if desired.

CHEWY PISTACHIO SLICE

One of my favourite biscuits from childhood is mamoul, on which this recipe is based. I recollect that it used to take my nana forever to make mamoul, so I have created a much simpler version of it that I think tastes just as good as the original.

BASE

160 g (5½ oz) plain (all-purpose) flour
75 g (2½ oz/⅓ cup) caster (superfine)
   sugar
120 g (4¼ oz) cold butter, cut into cubes

TOPPING

4 eggs
285 g (10 oz/1½ cups, lightly packed)
   dark brown sugar
1 teaspoon natural vanilla extract
4 tablespoons plain (all-purpose) flour
1 teaspoon ground cinnamon
2 teaspoons baking powder
½ teaspoon salt
400 g (14 oz/4 cups) pistachio nut
   kernels, coarsely chopped
icing (confectioners') sugar, to dust

Preheat the oven to 170°C (325°F). Line a 20 cm x 30 cm (8 inch x 12 inch) baking tin with baking paper.

To make the base, put the flour, sugar and butter in a food processor and pulse until the mixture resembles breadcrumbs. Spread the mixture evenly over the base of the tin and press in lightly. Bake for 20 minutes, or until golden brown.

To make the topping, put the eggs, sugar, vanilla, flour, cinnamon, baking powder, salt and pistachios in a large bowl and combine with your hands. Spread the mixture evenly over the base and bake for 20–25 minutes, until the topping feels firm.

Cool in the tin on a wire rack, then cut into small bars and serve dusted with icing sugar.

LAYERED KATAIFI, MASCARPONE AND FRESH BERRIES

Based on an Eton Mess, this spectacular dessert combines the lovely crunch of kataifi pastry with luscious cream and seasonal berries. The separate elements can be prepared ahead of time and then assembled just before serving to make an impressive dish with minimum effort. Rather than trying to cut it, scoop out each portion with a large spoon and serve in bowls.

250 g (9 oz) kataifi pastry

70 g (2½ oz) butter, melted

2 tablespoons caster (superfine) sugar

oil spray for greasing

500 g (1 lb 2 oz) mascarpone cheese

50 g (1¾ oz) icing (confectioners') sugar, plus 2 tablespoons extra

250 ml (9 fl oz/1 cup) thin (pouring) cream

800 g (1 lb 12 oz) mixed fresh berries

2–3 tablespoons pomegranate molasses (optional)

Put the kataifi pastry in a large mixing bowl and separate the strands with your hands. Add the melted butter and caster sugar and mix well by hand. Divide the mixture into 3 equal parts. Preheat the oven to 170°C (325°F).

Spray a 20 cm (8 inch) round cake tin well with oil. Take one portion of the kataifi mixture and spread it over the base of the tin, pushing it in and flattening it so the base is completely covered. Bake for 15–20 minutes, until the disc is light golden. Remove carefully from the tin and cool on a wire rack. Repeat with the remaining 2 portions so you have 3 baked discs.

To make the filling, put the mascarpone cheese, 50 g of icing sugar and the cream in a large bowl. Whisk together until thick and well combined, taking care not to overmix.

In a separate bowl, combine the mixed berries, the remaining icing sugar and the pomegranate molasses, if using, and carefully mix to combine, taking care not to crush the berries.

Assemble the dish on a serving platter or cake stand just before serving. Put 1 disc on the plate and top with a few spoonfuls of the mascarpone cream, pushing it almost to the edge of the disc, and scatter over a third of the berries. Add the second disc and repeat with more mascarpone cream and another third of the berries. Top with the last disc and the remaining mascarpone cream and berries.

CLASSIC KEPOS CARROT CUPCAKES

A great carrot cake recipe is an essential in everyone's baking repertoire, and I can vouch for the popularity of this one. We make these cupcakes for the café but you can use the recipe to make two 20 cm (8 inch) cakes and sandwich them with the topping.

2 large carrots, grated
200 g (7 oz) dark brown sugar
150 ml (5 fl oz) light olive oil
2 eggs
100 g (3½ oz) walnuts, coarsely
  chopped
175 g (6 oz) self-raising flour, sifted
½ teaspoon bicarbonate of soda
  (baking soda)
½ teaspoon ground cinnamon
½ teaspoon ground ginger
½ teaspoon freshly grated nutmeg
½ teaspoon salt

TOPPING
150 g (5½ oz) cream cheese, at room
  temperature
300 g (10½ oz) icing (confectioners')
  sugar, sifted
zest of 1 lemon

Preheat the oven to 180°C (350°F). Line the holes of a muffin tray with 8 large or 12 small paper cases.

Put the carrot, sugar, olive oil and eggs in a large bowl and mix well to combine. Add the walnuts and fold through.

Put the flour, bicarbonate of soda, cinnamon, ginger, nutmeg and salt in a medium bowl and mix well. Gradually add the dry ingredients to the carrot mixture, stirring with a wooden spoon until just combined. Spoon the mixture into the paper cases and bake for 25–30 minutes.

Remove the cupcakes from the tray and cool on a wire rack. Meanwhile, using an electric mixer with the paddle attachment, beat the cream cheese until smooth. Gradually add the icing sugar and lemon zest and beat until combined. Spoon a dollop of the cream cheese icing onto each cupcake.

CHOCOLATE AND CARDAMOM CAKE

Chocolate and cardamom is a beautiful combination, and this is a great cake for people with a gluten intolerance.

400 g (14 oz) dark chocolate, coarsely chopped
250 g (9 oz) unsalted butter
6 eggs
400 g (14 oz) caster (superfine) sugar
120 g (4¼ oz) almond meal
½ teaspoon ground cardamom
20 g (¾ oz) unsweetened cocoa powder, to dust
cream or ice cream, to serve

Preheat the oven to 180°C (350°F). Grease a 24 cm (9½ in) springform cake tin and line the base with baking paper.

Put the chocolate and butter in a bowl and melt in the microwave. Set aside to cool at room temperature.

Use an electric mixer with a whisk attachment to whisk the eggs and sugar until light and fluffy. Add the chocolate and fold in gently. Add the almond meal and cardamom and fold through.

Pour the mixture into the prepared tin. Bake for 40 minutes, or until the cake has a nice firm crust but is still slightly wobbly in the middle.

Cool in the tin on a wire rack. When cool, remove the springform ring and put the cake on a serving plate. Dust with the sifted cocoa powder.

Serve the cake at room temperature with fresh cream or ice cream, or reheat it. Store the cake in a cool place but not the fridge, as it will set and become too firm.

ALMOND AND COCONUT CAKE

Beautifully moist and with the taste of almonds, this cake can be made in advance for a dinner party, or enjoyed for afternoon tea. It keeps refrigerated for up to a week, but I'm not sure it will last that long.

6 eggs

300 g (10½ oz) unsalted butter, melted

270 g (9½ oz/2⅔ cups) almond meal

90 g (3¼ oz/1 cup) desiccated coconut

380 g (13½ oz) caster (superfine) sugar

½ teaspoon salt

1 vanilla bean, split lengthways and seeds scraped, or 1 tablespoon vanilla bean paste

50 g (1¾ oz/½ cup) almond flakes

Icing (confectioners') sugar, for dusting

Preheat the oven to 170°C (325°F). Grease a 24 cm (9½ inch) springform cake tin and line the base with baking paper.

Put the eggs in a large bowl and whisk with a fork. Add the butter and mix until combined.

Put the almond meal, coconut, sugar, salt and vanilla bean seeds in a medium bowl and mix to combine. Add the almond meal mixture to the egg mixture and mix well. Pour into the cake tin and scatter the almond flakes over the top. Bake for 45 minutes, or until the cake is firm and golden brown.

Cool the cake in the tin on a wire rack for 10 minutes. Remove the springform ring and allow the cake to cool completely. Dust with icing sugar to serve.

CHOCOLATE HALVA BROWNIES

I love these addictive brownies. They combine two of my favourite sweet ingredients – dark chocolate and sweet gooey halva – so I try to make them as often as possible.

350 g (12 oz) plain halva, cut into
   2 cm (¾ inch) cubes
200 g (7 oz) dark chocolate,
   coarsely chopped
150 g (5½ oz) unsalted butter,
   coarsely chopped
4 eggs
300 g (10½ oz) caster (superfine) sugar
140 g (5 oz) plain (all-purpose) flour
20 g (¾ oz) unsweetened
   cocoa powder
½ teaspoon salt

Line a 20 cm x 30 cm (8 inch x 12 inch) baking tin with baking paper. Scatter the halva cubes evenly over the base of the tin.

Put the chocolate and butter in a heatproof bowl over a saucepan of simmering water, not letting the water touch the base of the bowl. Stir until melted. Alternatively, melt the chocolate and butter in a microwave. Set aside.

Put the eggs and sugar in a large bowl and whisk until the sugar has dissolved. Slowly pour the melted chocolate mixture over the egg mixture and stir until combined.

Sift the flour, cocoa powder and salt over the chocolate mixture and gently fold through. Pour the chocolate mixture over the halva cubes and gently spread over the base of the baking tin. Set aside to rest at room temperature for 30 minutes (this helps give the brownies a better crust). Preheat the oven to 180°C (350°F).

Bake the brownies for 20–25 minutes, or until they are set but still gooey in the centre. Cool on a wire rack. When completely cool, cut into 16 pieces.

STORAGE
Store in an airtight container for up to 1 week or freeze for up to 1 month.

LAYERED TURKISH DELIGHT PAVLOVA

I always struggle to find light desserts to serve at the end of a meal as most people tend to like chocolate-based desserts. The pink grapefruit in this pavlova has a lovely bitter flavour that cuts through the sweetness of the meringue and balances a rich meal. If you don't like the bitterness of the grapefruit you can substitute orange or any other citrus, but I suggest giving it a try as I think you'll be pleasantly surprised.

oil spray for greasing

7 egg whites, at room temperature

375 g (13 oz) caster (superfine) sugar

2 tablespoons white vinegar

1 tablespoon rosewater

250 g (9 oz) mascarpone cheese

250 ml (9 fl oz/1 cup) thin (pouring) cream

50 g (1¾ oz) icing (confectioners') sugar

4–5 pink grapefruit, segmented (see below)

300 g (10½ oz) good-quality Turkish delight, finely chopped

3 tablespoons pistachio nuts, lightly toasted and crushed

edible dried rose petals, to garnish

Preheat the oven to 160°C (320°F). Spray a 20 x 30 cm (8 x 12 inch) cake tin with oil and line with baking paper.

Using an electric mixer fitted with a whisk attachment, whisk the egg whites for 2–3 minutes, until soft peaks form. With the machine running, slowly add the caster sugar and then whisk for a further 8–10 minutes, until firm and glossy. Use a metal spoon to fold in the vinegar and rosewater.

Spoon the meringue mixture into the prepared tin and smooth the top. Bake for exactly 20 minutes, then remove from the oven and set aside to cool completely. Don't worry if the meringue looks a bit rustic when you take it out of the oven.

Put the mascarpone, cream and icing sugar in a large bowl and whisk until soft peaks form.

To assemble, cut the meringue in half so there are two 20 x 15 cm (8 x 6 inch) pieces. Put one piece on a serving plate and top with half the mascarpone mixture, half the grapefruit segments and half the Turkish delight. Top with the remaining meringue, then the remaining mascarpone mixture, grapefruit and Turkish delight. Scatter the pistachios and rose petals over the top.

HOW TO SEGMENT CITRUS
Cut off the top and bottom of the citrus fruit. Using a sharp knife, carefully remove the skin and white pith, following the line of the fruit. Remove each segment by slicing either side of the membrane. It is good to do this over a bowl to capture any juice that comes out of the fruit.

KEPOS STREET CHURROS

Churros are a Kepos Street Kitchen signature. They've been on the menu since we opened in 2012 and I don't think our customers would let us take them off. This is a great dessert to serve for a group of people as the batter can be made in advance. Serve the churros immediately once they are cooked. We serve them in a paper bag with the cinnamon sugar. Our customers shake the bag around to coat the churros and there is nothing better than the smell of the warm churros and cinnamon.

200 ml (7 fl oz) buttermilk
100 g (3½ oz) unsalted butter
1 tablespoon caster (superfine) sugar
½ teaspoon salt
seeds of 1 vanilla bean
300 g (10½ oz/2 cups) plain
    (all-purpose) flour, sifted
4 large eggs
vegetable oil or rice bran oil,
    for deep-frying

CINNAMON SUGAR
200 g (7 oz) caster (superfine) sugar
1 teaspoon ground cinnamon

Combine the buttermilk, butter, sugar, salt, vanilla seeds and 125 ml (4 fl oz/½ cup) of water in a saucepan. Bring to the boil over medium heat, then reduce the heat to low. Slowly add the flour, stirring with a wooden spoon until it has all been incorporated. Cook, stirring constantly, for a further 10 minutes. Remove from the heat and set aside to cool for 5 minutes.

Transfer the batter to an electric mixer with a paddle attachment and beat on medium speed for 2 minutes. Slowly add the eggs, one at a time, and beat until they are incorporated into the batter (you may need to reduce the mixer speed when adding the eggs). Increase the speed and beat for 2–3 minutes, until the batter is smooth and no longer sticks to the side of the bowl.

Spoon the batter into a piping (icing) bag with a star nozzle.

To make the cinnamon sugar, mix the sugar and cinnamon together in a bowl. Set aside.

Using a deep-fryer or a large deep saucepan, heat the oil to 170°C (340°F). If you don't have a thermometer, drop in a cube of bread – the oil is hot enough when the bread turns golden brown in 20 seconds. Pipe 10 cm (4 inch) lengths of the batter into the oil and cook in batches for 3–4 minutes, until golden. Remove the churros with a slotted spoon, drop them into the cinnamon sugar and turn to coat. Serve warm.

NOTE
The churros are lovely served with store-bought dulce de leche or caramel, with a sprinkle of sea salt flakes.

MUHALBIYAH WITH ROSEWATER (MILK PUDDING)

There was a food stand close to my childhood home that sold nothing but muhalbiyah. We kids loved the sugar rush we'd get from the cheap and tacky syrup with its artificial colouring, while the adults had a version made with grenadine syrup. Mine is a more sophisticated adult version, but still based on this childhood memory.

1 litre (35 fl oz/4 cups) full-cream (whole) milk
80 g (2¾ oz) caster (superfine) sugar
70 g (2½ oz) cornflour (cornstarch)
2 tablespoons rosewater
100 g (3½ oz/¾ cup) pistachio nut kernels, toasted and coarsely chopped, to serve
fresh raspberries, to serve

SAUCE
300 g (10½ oz) fresh or frozen raspberries
50 g (1¾ oz) caster (superfine) sugar
1 tablespoon rosewater

Put the milk and sugar in a medium saucepan over medium–low heat and bring to the boil. Meanwhile, put the cornflour in a small bowl and add a few tablespoons of water, stirring until you have a gluggy wet mixture. Slowly add the cornflour to the hot milk, stirring with a wooden spoon, and reduce the temperature to low. Continue stirring for 8–10 minutes, or until the mixture has the consistency of a thick custard. Add the rosewater, stir and remove from the heat.

Pour the mixture into 4–6 serving glasses and allow to cool to room temperature. Transfer to the fridge and set overnight.

To make the sauce, put the raspberries and sugar in a food processor or blender and purée until smooth. Pass through a fine-mesh sieve to remove the seeds. Put the liquid in a small saucepan over low heat and bring to the boil. Simmer for 5 minutes then remove from the heat. Add the rosewater, stir and allow to cool.

When you are ready to serve, pour the sauce over the puddings and scatter with the pistachios and raspberries.

Serves 8

ORANGE AND HAZELNUT TEA CAKE

Polenta cakes may sound complicated to make but they really are a simple gluten-free option. Most polenta recipes tend to use almond meal but I've used hazelnut meal as it gives the cake a much deeper colour and a nuttier flavour. It's lovely served with plain Greek-style yoghurt to balance the sweetness and richness of the orange syrup.

180 g (6 oz) butter, at room temperature
230 g (8 oz) caster (superfine) sugar
seeds of 1 vanilla bean
grated zest and juice of 2 oranges
3 large eggs
180 g (6 oz) hazelnut meal
100 g (3½ oz) instant polenta
1 teaspoon baking powder

GARNISH

2 oranges
110 g (3¾ oz/½ cup) caster (superfine)
    sugar
185 ml (6 fl oz/¾ cup) water
50 g (1¾ oz/⅓ cup) hazelnuts,
    lightly toasted

Preheat the oven to 160°C (320°F). Lightly grease a 24 cm (9½ inch) springform cake tin and line the base with baking paper.

Using an electric mixer with a paddle attachment, whisk the butter and 180 g (6 oz) of the sugar with the vanilla seeds and orange zest until light and fluffy, about 5 minutes. Add the eggs and whisk until combined.

While the mixer is running, combine the hazelnut meal, polenta and baking powder. Pour the mixture over the butter mixture and mix on low speed until combined.

Spoon the mixture into the prepared tin and bake for 40–45 minutes, until lightly golden and cooked through when tested with a skewer.

While the cake is cooking, prepare the garnish. Peel the oranges using a vegetable peeler, then slice the peel thinly. Place the sugar and water in a saucepan over low to medium heat and simmer until sugar has completely dissolved. Add the strips of orange peel and cook for 4–5 minutes until they have softened up.

Remove the saucepan from the heat and set aside until ready to use.

Cool the cake in the tin for at least 5 minutes before turning out onto a wire rack. Spoon the syrup and strips of peel over the cake. Finish with the toasted hazelnuts.

Kitchen Fundamentals

Master these simple cooking techniques for the perfect result, every time.

HOW TO COOK COUSCOUS

SERVES 4

190 g (6¾ oz/1 cup) couscous
2–3 tablespoons olive oil
310 ml (10¾ fl oz/1¼ cups) boiling water or stock

Put the couscous in a stainless steel bowl and drizzle the oil over it. Gently rub the grains with your fingertips so they are coated with the oil, which will help give you a fluffier, less gluggy couscous.

Add the boiling water, season to taste with salt and stir to combine. Tightly cover the bowl with plastic wrap and allow the couscous to steam for 10–15 minutes.

When the couscous has absorbed the water, fluff it up with a fork and serve.

NOTE

For a savoury couscous, add a teaspoon of seasoning, such as ground turmeric, cumin or coriander, when you are rubbing the couscous with the oil. For a sweeter version, add a dash of vanilla sugar, or a pinch of ground cinnamon or freshly grated nutmeg, after the couscous has cooled and been fluffed.

HOW TO COOK POLENTA

Makes a 20 cm x 20 cm (8 inch x 8 inch) tray

800 ml (28 fl oz) full-cream (whole) milk
20 g (¾ oz) butter
1 teaspoon sea salt flakes
200 g (7 oz) instant polenta

Line a 20 cm (8 inch) square baking tin with baking paper.

Put the milk, butter and salt in a medium saucepan over medium–high heat and bring to the boil. Once boiling, whisk in the polenta slowly until the mixture binds together. Change to a wooden spoon and stir until the polenta becomes firm but not too hard.

Spread the polenta evenly into the lined tin. Allow to cool in the fridge for at least 3 hours.

When ready to grill or pan-fry, turn the polenta out onto a chopping board, remove the baking paper and cut to the desired size and shape.

HOW TO COOK RICE

Serves 4 as a side dish

olive oil, for coating
200 g (7 oz/1 cup) basmati rice
375 ml (13 fl oz/1½ cups) boiling water or stock

Place a saucepan with a lid over medium heat. Add enough olive oil to coat the bottom of the saucepan. Add the rice and stir to coat with the oil.

Cook until the grains are toasted then add the water or stock. Add salt to taste and bring to the boil.

Once boiling, put the lid on the saucepan and turn the heat down to the lowest setting. Cook with the lid on for 18 minutes.

Remove the saucepan from the heat and allow to rest for 5 minutes, keeping the lid on.

Remove the lid, fluff the grains with a fork and serve.

NOTE
The rice can be flavoured by adding 1 teaspoon of ground turmeric or a pinch of saffron threads when toasting it. Or add a makrut lime leaf or a chunk of ginger when the water or stock has been added.

HOW TO STERILISE JARS & BOTTLES

To sterilise jars and bottles for storing jams, chutneys or mayonnaise, preheat the oven to 150°C (300°F).

Wash the glassware in warm soapy water, rinse and put it in the oven for 15–20 minutes, until completely dry. Place the lids in a saucepan of boiling water and boil for 10 minutes. Remove with tongs and leave to dry on a clean tea towel (dish towel).

Building Your Pantry

The spices, seeds, grains and pulses that follow, as well as the kitchen fundamentals in the previous pages, are the building blocks I recommend for enjoying this style of cooking and eating. Most of the spices, blends and other ingredients will be available at the local supermarket, but if there is a Middle Eastern grocery store nearby, all the better. For equipment, a sharp knife and chopping board, a basic set of pots and pans, serving plates and bowls, and a working stove and oven should pretty much do it.

SPICES

It is worth investigating whether there is a Middle Eastern or Mediterranean grocery store in your area so you can buy all of the ingredients you need in the one place. With spices, I like to buy the whole seeds and then toast and grind them as required, as toasting brings out the flavour of the spices and makes them more fragrant. Most are best stored in an airtight container in a cool, dark cupboard, and will last several months if kept this way.

Allspice Berry

A berry from an evergreen tree, allspice is picked and dried before it ripens. According to Jane Lawson's *Spice Market*, 'Allspice is considered Mother Nature's spice mix in a single berry'. If you can't find allspice, a good substitute is equal parts of cinnamon and mace, then half parts of cloves and pepper.

USES: Allspice is used a lot in savoury Middle Eastern dishes with rice and minced (ground) meat.

Baharat

A mixture that varies from region to region but will often include cinnamon or cassia bark, cumin, cardamom, nutmeg and cloves. The word 'baharat' means 'spice' in Arabic.

USES: As a dry rub for meats.

Caraway Seed

Also known as Persian cumin, the seeds come from an umbelliferous flower and have aniseed notes, and warm and aromatic flavours. Dry-roasting before use brings out the oils and the flavours. They can be used whole or ground.

USES: Good for flavouring breads, casseroles, desserts and liqueurs.

Cardamom

The green and black/brown cardamom are separate species of the ginger family. In Arab countries cardamom is mainly used as a flavouring for coffee and the seeds are chewed to freshen breath.

USES: Green cardamom is mostly used for flavouring desserts and teas, and black/brown cardamom – which is coarser in taste – is used more in meat and vegetable dishes. The seeds rather than the whole pods are traditionally chewed.

Cassia

Resembling cinnamon and sold similarly in sticks (quills) and in powdered form, cassia is reddish-brown in colour and has a much more robust flavour than cinnamon.

USES: Use as for cinnamon but expect a robust rather than delicate flavour.

Chillies

There are more than 300 varieties of chilli from five main species.

USES: For an extra kick in Middle Eastern cooking.

Cinnamon

A common and ever-popular spice, cinnamon comes from an evergreen tree related to the laurel or bay leaf family. It comes in stick (quill) and powdered forms.

USES: Cinnamon is used in Middle Eastern tagines and other slow-cooked dishes.

Coriander Seed

Coriander seed is the dried ripe seed of the plant that gives us the fresh herb. It is available in seed and powdered form, and has been used as a spice since ancient times.

USES: It is mainly used in savoury cooking but also works well with apples and can be used in cakes.

Cumin Seed

The cumin plant is a member of the parsley family, and its dried ripe seeds – which can be dry-roasted whole or ground to a powder – have an earthy and slightly bitter flavour.

USES: Mainly used in Mediterranean cooking but with many applications in Middle Eastern dishes.

Fennel Seed

Wild fennel is used for seeds (the other varieties are for fennel used as a vegetable). Arab spice traders took this seed from the Mediterranean to the Middle East, then later to East Asia and India. If fennel and dill are grown near each other they will cross-pollinate.

USES: Used in spice mixes, tagines, bastilla and fish dishes, and also in desserts.

Fenugreek

The spice is the dried ripe seed of the fenugreek plant, which is a member of the pea and clover family. Its aroma resembles celery, and when roasted it smells like burnt sugar or maple. It needs slow-roasting to bring out its flavour fully but overheating makes the seeds taste bitter.

USES: Often used in spice blends, curries and oils, and can be used in desserts.

Mastic

The sap or resin from the mastic (also known as the lentisk) tree or shrub. It comes in hard crystalline lumps and is often crushed before use.

USES: Often paired with rosewater and used to make Turkish delight, as well as desserts, breads, ice cream and puddings, and to add flavour to stews.

Nutmeg

Along with mace, this spice comes from the nutmeg tree and is available whole or powdered.

USES: Used with meat, rice and desserts, and mixed with sugar. It's best to use it freshly grated.

Paprika

The familiar pungent red spice is the dried ground fruit of *Capsicum annuum*, the mild capsicum fruit often called pimento. It exists in many varieties, some of them very hot. 'Regular' paprika is normally mild and sweet and can be used generously. Smoked paprika gets its distinctive smoky flavour from a slow drying process over oak-burning fires.

USES: Mostly used in stews, when it is often mixed with flour, but also good with many meats and fish, and in marinades and dressings.

Saffron

Prized since the dawn of civilisation, saffron is the dried stigma of a flower from the crocus family. It is quite expensive because of the complex harvesting process involved.

USES: Used in rice dishes, tagines and stews, and in dressings and desserts. You need only a small amount when cooking. In *The Spice Book*, Arabella Boxer explains how to maximise the flavour of saffron: gently toast it over low heat, then crush using a mortar and pestle, add a couple of spoonfuls of hot liquid such as stock or water and leave to infuse for 5 minutes.

Sesame Seeds

Reportedly one of the oldest seeds consumed by humans according to Jane Lawson's *Spice Market*, which also reveals an interesting fact: 'Plants are harvested prior to being fully ripe, as when ripe they spontaneously shatter. This act of nature is said to be the basis of the phrase "open sesame" from *The Arabian Nights*.' Sesame seeds are very nutritious but also high in kilojoules/calories because they comprise about 50 per cent oil.

USES: Sesame seeds are ground to make tahini and used in spice blends (for example dukkah), falafel, desserts or as a garnish in Middle Eastern cooking. They are used quite differently in Asian cuisine.

Star Anise

Woody and aniseed in flavour, and beautiful to look at, star anise comes from an evergreen tree in the same family as magnolias. Its shape is an eight-pointed star, and it is said to be 13 times sweeter than sugar.

USES: Used in teas, marinades, spice blends, stews and desserts.

Sumac

Sumac is the dried fruit of a shrub related to the cashew tree. It is ground into a powder that is sour and tart in flavour. It was originally a source of citrus flavour for the Egyptians in their cooking. Packaged sumac may contain salt to help preserve its flavour.

USES: Features in za'atar and is used in marinades and dressings, in breads and as a garnish.

Turmeric

A member of the ginger family, this brightly coloured spice is also known as 'poor man's saffron'. Turmeric imparts an earthy flavour, is a natural antiseptic and is good to use for preserving. Best purchased in its ground form.

USES: Used in chermoula, and to add an earthy flavour to savoury dishes.

Vanilla

The vanilla pod is the fruit of a climbing orchid from Central America. It is the second most expensive spice in the world after saffron – expensive because of the processes involved in turning the fresh pod into a dried bean. You can make your own vanilla essence by splitting a vanilla bean and soaking it in pure alcohol, such as vodka, for 2–3 weeks.

USES: Great in sweet dishes.

GRAINS & PULSES

I like to buy my supplies from Middle Eastern grocery stores as I know they will have all that I need and the turnover of their products will be high. Transfer your bags of grains and pulses to airtight containers as soon as you get them home, and store them in a cool, dark place.

Barley

This member of the grass family is one of the earliest cultivated plants. Pearl barley is the most common form.

USES: Mostly used in soups and salads but can also be used for desserts.

Burghul

Its name is the Persian word for 'bruised grain', and it is also known as bulgur wheat. It has a light, nutty flavour and is actually wheat that has been cooked, had its bran removed, and been dried and then ground into grains.

USES: Burghul is one of the main ingredients in tabouleh and kibbeh.

Chickpeas

A type of pod, with each containing 2–3 peas, this small legume dates back to 800 BC. There are three types of chickpeas but the kabuli variety is the one most commonly used in Middle Eastern and Mediterranean cooking. Chickpeas are high in protein and an important food in many parts of the world. Dried chickpeas need soaking prior to cooking but the tinned form are cooked. Chickpeas can be processed to make chickpea flour, or besan.

USES: The main ingredient in hummus, chickpeas are also used in salads and tagines, and can be roasted and eaten as a snack.

Couscous

Traditionally made from freshly ground whole grain, but not a 'grain' as such, couscous is made of tiny little balls of dough. To make it at home, start with a bowl of semolina flour sprinkled with salted water. Rake your fingers through the flour in a sweeping round motion, which causes the dough to form tiny balls. The balls are then dried, steamed and separated again to create the 'grains'. There are various kinds, including popular pre-cooked 'instant' couscous, and the larger-grained 'giant' couscous varieties, such as pearl, Israeli and moghrabieh.

USES: Used in both savoury and sweet dishes.

Freekeh

Freekah is made by harvesting green wheat, roasting it and then cracking it. Freekeh is commonly referred to as an ancient grain, and it is thought to date back to around 2300 BC, when a town in the Eastern Mediterranean came under siege. To prevent imminent starvation, the townsfolk harvested their crops early and stored the green wheat, but the stockpiles caught on fire and the outer grains were burnt. However, people found that rubbing the burnt wheat heads together revealed the toasted grains inside, and they called this freekeh, which means 'the rubbed one'. It's very popular in Middle Eastern and North African cuisines.

USES: Used in salads and soups.

Lentils

Growing on a small bushy plant in pods that contain 1–2 seeds, lentils are the best-known members of the legume family. There are numerous kinds, varying in size, colour, flavour and length of cooking time necessary, including red, green and brown, and the small French, or puy, lentil. They are low in fat, and high in protein and fibre, and an important food source in many cultures.

USES: Used in soups, salads, stews and patties.

Split Dried Broad Beans

When dried and split, broad beans develop a nutty flavour.

USES: Roasted as a snack or used to make falafel, dips, stews, curries and soups.

Acknowledgments

Creating these cookbooks has been an amazing experience and there are many people to thank.

To our families and friends who have always been supportive, keep us laughing and evolving, and are always happy to come over to our home for a shared meal. Thank you for being our cheerleaders.

A big thank you to the Kepos staff, past and present, who contributed in many ways to all cookbooks. Your ideas, creativity and feedback – invaluable. Your backup at work allowed us the time to spend on the books.

The team at Murdoch Books has been amazing to work with. Thank you for believing in us the first time round with *Falafel for Breakfast,* then letting us come back for seconds with *Hummus & Co* and now with the best-of book, *Middle Eastern Feasts*. Thank you to the past Murdoch team including Sue Hines for believing in us as new authors and Lou Johnson for taking over where Sue left off. Murdoch Books allowed us an amazing amount of freedom. Corinne Roberts was always there to bounce off ideas, offer suggestions and comments and most importantly give feedback with our recipe testing! It takes so many people to bring an idea to life. We loved the creation of the beautiful pages with a design and colour palette that complemented our food.

Thanks to Justin Wolfers, our new guiding light at Murdoch, who developed the concept for this new book. We've loved working with you on *Middle Eastern Feasts*; watch this space for our next book, coming soon. Thanks as well to Sarah Odgers, Sarah McCoy, Breanna Blundell and Julie Mazur Tribe for helping bring this new edition together.

Alan Benson is like a friend who is an amazing photographer and we are just casually getting together to create a few books. We have so much fun working with you and there is more fun to be had with the new book. You are creative and extremely passionate and this is reflected in the beautiful images. We love these photos.

The photographer brings to life the beautiful work of the talented stylists, Jane Hann (*Falafel for Breakfast*) and Bernie Smithies (*Hummus & Co*), making the food shine on the pages.

We've hosted a lot of people while working on these cookbooks, so thanks to all our taste testers. We know it can be hard to try all that delicious food but someone has to do it!

Thank you to Terry Durack and Jill Dupleix for the introduction to Murdoch Books and then for inviting us back for seconds. Without your valuable food knowledge we would not have been able to collaborate on two books as well as future projects. We are flattered that you felt the world needed to see more recipes from us.

And lastly, thank you to our parents for believing in us and for your unwavering support. You are our number 1 fans, and even if one of you is no longer with us, you've always been there for us and are passionate about everything we do.

Michael Rantissi & Kristy Frawley

Index

D

Published in 2024 by Murdoch Books, an imprint of Allen & Unwin

Murdoch Books Australia
Cammeraygal Country
83 Alexander Street
Crows Nest NSW 2065
Phone: +61 (0)2 8425 0100
murdochbooks.com.au
info@murdochbooks.com.au

Murdoch Books UK
Ormond House
26–27 Boswell Street
London WC1N 3JZ
Phone: +44 (0) 20 8785 5995
murdochbooks.co.uk
info@murdochbooks.co.uk

For corporate orders and custom publishing, contact our business development team at
salesenquiries@murdochbooks.com.au

Publisher: Justin Wolfers
Editorial manager and project editor: Breanna Blundell
Design manager: Sarah Odgers
Designer and cover designer: Sarah McCoy
Photographer: Alan Benson
Stylists: Jane Hann, Berni Smithies
Home economists: Ross Dobson, Claire Dickson-Smith
Production director: Lou Playfair

Murdoch Books acknowledges the Traditional Owners of the Country on which we live and work.
We pay our respects to all Aboriginal and Torres Strait Islander Elders, past and present.

Recipes in this book have been previously published in *Falafel for Breakfast* and *Hummus and Co*.

ISBN 978 1 76150 039 8

A catalogue record for this book is available from the National Library of Australia

A catalogue record for this book is available from the British Library

Colour reproduction by Splitting Image Colour Studio Pty Ltd, Wantirna, Victoria
Printed by 1010 Printing International Limited, China

OVEN GUIDE: You may find cooking times vary depending on the oven you are using. For fan-forced ovens, as a general rule, set the oven temperature to 20°C (35°F) lower than indicated in the recipe.

IMPORTANT: Those who might be at risk from the effects of salmonella poisoning (the elderly, pregnant women, young children and those suffering from immune deficiency diseases) should consult their doctor with any concerns about eating raw lamb.

TABLESPOON MEASURES: We have used 20 ml (4 teaspoon) tablespoon measures. If you are using a 15 ml (3 teaspoon) tablespoon add an extra teaspoon of the ingredient for each tablespoon specified.

10 9 8 7 6 5 4 3 2 1

MIX
Paper | Supporting responsible forestry
FSC® C016973